Between Heaven

and

A Hard Place

A Divine Paradox

by

Dr. Stew Bittman

LionHearted Publishing,® Inc.
Zephyr Cove, NV 89448

LionHearted Publishing,® Inc.
P.O. Box 618
Zephyr Cove, NV 89448-0618
888-546-6478

Email us at **admin@LionHearted.com**

Visit our web site at **www.LionHearted.com**

Cover design: M.A. Heathman

Library of Congress Control Number: 2004109326

ISBN: 1-57343-060-9

Printed in the U.S.A.

To Hillary and Ari

Acknowledgements

To my many teachers, including Dr. Jim Parker (may he rest in peace), Dr. Dick Santo, Dr. Cecil Collins, Dr. Reggie Gold, Dr. John Demartini, Dr. Dean Black, and especially, Dr. Jim Sigafoose: my deepest gratitude for your wisdom and your willingness to share it.

To my chiropractic family: my sincerest appreciation for your support and for your passion.

To my many practice folks over the years: my undying regards for putting up with me and for all the blessings you *brot* me.

To my birth family: my humblest thanks for your unconditional love and for your great humor in helping to shape my life and my gifts.

To my wife, Hillary, and my daughter, Arielle: my grandest love for your patience *thru* this process, for your help with it, and, most of all, for the sweetness, joy, and light you both bring into my world.

Introduction

I recently read *thru* my first book and the words are only vaguely familiar. They make me laugh and cry and sometimes cringe. I notice I am just beginning to truly live and experience some of the things I wrote about so confidently years ago. I suppose I was writing by faith, not by sight. I'm happy to be catching up. Undoubtedly, I'll be saying the same things about this book someday.

That being said, a word or four of caution before we proceed. There is little contained herein that could be described as progressing in a linear or even logical manner. The same can be said, however, about my life. Also, *tho* I take great pride in the fact that I am rather proficient in the lost art of spelling, you may notice — as spell check certainly did — I misspell words like "thought" and "brought" *thru-out* the book. I have followed the example of B.J. Palmer, the Developer of Chiropractic, and removed the "ugh" from these words.

Speaking of "ugh," the word "Schmootz" which literally means "dirt" in Yiddish, has been substituted for the word "shit" in my vernacular.

I have dedicated my life to uncovering this place that lies within all of us and represents our refuge, our safe haven, from the storms of illusion that our minds create. When you and I are in that place, we are indeed one. Finding that place and then living from that place are the most important things we can ever do, for ourselves and for the world.

Finally, while much of what you read is not "serious" and may often border on nonsense and near blasphemy, please keep in mind that nearly every word came from a place within me that is as real as I get. It's a place that represents my highest truth. *I have dedicated my life to uncovering this place that lies within all of us and represents our refuge, our safe haven, from the storms of illusion that our minds create. When you and I are in that place, we are indeed one. Finding that place and then living from that place are the most important things we can ever do, for ourselves and for the world.*

This book is a travelogue of my ongoing journey from a hard place to my heart. I offer my journey to Spirit as a gift. I hope that by witnessing my struggles to become whole, you will allow yourself the same permission. As I share my attempts to obliterate my ego, and ultimately to make peace with it *thru* laughter and tears, sense and nonsense, may you find the freedom to love all your pieces.

Thank you for joining me.

Stew Bittman

Chapter <0: (Less than "0")

Somewhere Between Paradoxes?

"He may look like an idiot and talk like an idiot,
but don't let that fool you. He really is an idiot."
Groucho Marx

So where am I now?

My mind, my ego, and my programming, which I generally refer to collectively as the *"Schmootz Brigade,"* all have their own opinions. They have me bouncing somewhere between focusing on my chiropractic practice and traveling, speaking, writing, and teaching. Somewhere between here and there. Somewhere between being and doing. Somewhere between yesterday and tomorrow. Somewhere between heaven and earth. Somewhere between clinging to the last shreds of the illusion of control and surrendering. Somewhere between serving me and serving God. Somewhere between despair and hope, between anger and hysterical laughter, between confusion and clarity, as I observe the world and its apparent clueless-ness and chaos.

At times the *Schmootz Brigade* has me furtively roaming, without compass or watch, reckless of my bearings, yet absolutely captured in space and time. It ceaselessly beckons to lead me astray, pulling the wool over this moment's eyes, hoping I don't notice. It wants to keep me swimming in the quicksand of paradox.

If we acknowledge that our choices determine not only our lives, but the state of the planet as well, then it is time to reflect on how well we are doing.

There's a line in a Woody Allen movie, *Sleeper* I believe, in which Woody claims that everything our mothers told us was good for us is actually bad. He includes as examples the sun, milk, red meat and college. There's a ton of truth in there. And it's not that our mothers were wrong or had hurtful intentions. They simply shared with us the prevalent thinking of the time.

And the prevalent thinking of yesterday is a major source of humor today. Why is that? Why does the prevalent thinking change so rapidly and so often?

When I was a kid, the diet plate in restaurants consisted of a hamburger without the roll, a mound of cottage cheese, and a bowl of canned peaches in heavy syrup. Then, for many years, it was the roll and none of the other stuff. Now, the hamburger and the cottage cheese are finding their ways back onto diet plates around the globe. What's going on? Have our nutritional needs changed that much in the past 45 years? Or has something else changed? Which is true?

Nowhere else is this phenomenon more evident than in the realm of health and healthcare, where I tend to hang out most of the time. Breast-feeding is good. Nope, it's bad. Well... maybe it's not so bad after all. Circumcision? Was good for some, then good for all, now maybe not so good? In the past, when some kid on the block got the measles, the parents would get all the kids together for a measles party. Now, that's crazy. Let's put the kid in isolation. Better yet, let's make sure he or she *never* gets the measles by inoculating with measles vaccine. Maybe if we sterilized the universe we would never get sick! Hmmm? And then there's the disease of the month club. The popularity of rheumatism gave way to hypoglycemia, then candidiasis, and currently fibromyalgia. "Alternative" care, which for thousands of years was considered to be mainstream, is becoming mainstream again. Have these bodies and the best ways to take care of them changed that much? Or has something else changed? Which is true?

Our reliance on the current idea of "truth" becomes the basis for many, if not all, of our choices. *If we acknowledge that our choices determine not only our lives, but the state of the planet as well, then it is time to reflect on how well we are doing*. If the truth, as promised, will set us free, why are so many of us not free? Why is there so much suffering; so much hate, so much disease, so much disharmony, so much war? Is the problem not enough money or science or technology? Are we suffering from a lack of truth?

Reflecting on my own life, I would definitely say I suffered from a lack of truth. The prevalent thinking was always my truth. I was extremely well versed in it, and yet I always suspected there was something extremely important missing. My brain, by society's standards, was as good as anyone's, and the truth continued to simultaneously beckon and elude me.

Indeed, what is truth? Is it something for science to decide? Can the truth be determined with our minds? Is the truth, according to my mind, true for you as well? Is there any such thing as a fact? As I have explored my spirituality, the answers to these questions have bounced around like a Mexican jumping bean. There have been times of the utmost clarity and of the utmost confusion.

As my principled path brings me

*Love
has been my
metal detector
as I've tiptoed
thru the
minefields
of paradox
encountered
on the journey
from my head
to my heart.*

into another year, I notice that the things I see along the path, even the path itself, become less and less concrete. What is real? More and more the answer that comes is, "not much."

Everything in our society is so arbitrary!

The New Year's holiday was another reminder. Our beautiful green planet takes another trip around the sun, starting from and returning to some arbitrary spot in space, and we celebrate a new year. We argued over the "real" first day of the new millennium, while a billion or so Chinese didn't even think it was the first day of the year. My life revolves around things like a three-meal day, a seven-day week, a twelve-month year. My 40th birthday was somehow more important than my 43rd. All arbitrary!

The arbitrary-osity of things led me to look the word up in the dictionary, and Mr. Webster says, "left to one's discretion; regulated by one's own judgment or choice."

Most of my life I have chosen to accept all the countless myths fabricated out of someone else's judgment or choice, accepted by sufficient numbers of other people to become the deceptively real framework of my day-to-day existence. I became trapped in an illusionary structure of my own creation. I felt safe and secure in this fun house of cards and called it the "material" world, even *tho* it's all as arbitrary as which way to face the toilet paper—of course we all know it's supposed to face in.

Thru it all I have been confronted with paradoxes!

My brain whines and reels, seemingly blown in every direction by the paradoxes that it conjures up. It

I can choose to see the arbitrary nature of the material world...
and rely more and more on the spiritual world. On things that are real... chiropractic, friendship, love, God. And my connection to God, in chiropractic what we call "Innate Intelligence."

With love there are no paradoxes. With love I am finding my truth. And so will the world... and we will all be set free.

offers no solace, nor instructions for reconciling the paradoxes. It just keeps adding to the list, like an endless train careening off the tracks of my old belief systems and programming.

These paradoxes provide me with the raw materials I need to become increasingly grounded in Spirit. They force me to realize I can never reconcile them *thru* my intellect. They challenge me to open my heart. They empower me to see a bigger picture—to rest in the balance and perfection that always exists and is always manifesting—to look past the duality, past the good and bad, past the illusion, and find love.

Love has been my metal detector as I've tiptoed thru the minefields of paradox encountered on the journey from my head to my heart.

Regulated by my own judgment or choice, *I can choose to see the arbitrary nature of the material world,* which includes the *Schmootz Brigade,* and *I can rely more and more on the spiritual world. On things that are real.* Things like *chiropractic, friendship, love, God. And my connection to God, in chiropractic what we call "Innate Intelligence."*

The more I focus on these things, the better person I become, the better chiropractor I become, the more successful and aware I become.

Focusing on these things, I can awaken to the fact that my eyes and ears and brain generally deceive me. I can watch from a still and silent space, even when my brain and body are joining in mischievous and often downright ugly pranks with my ego. I can then take the illusion they represent and shake it by the scruff of its neck.

I realize that only some electrochemical activity in my brain is keeping me separate from everything I see and don't see, all of which is truly part of me. I can see arbitrary beliefs and filters are keeping me trapped in a trance; and in that trance I manifest all the expectations and attachments and jealousies and attacks and defenses that discolor my life and create all my suffering. I can even choose to change my electrochemical activity to align with the perfection that always exists in each moment.

I can and I do, sometimes.

With love there are no paradoxes. With love I am finding my truth. And so will the world… and we will all be set free.

So where am I now, really? I'll let you be the judge.

♥   ♥   ♥

*Neither
truth
nor facts
can be
considered
absolute.
Both are very
much relative
to common
experience,
consensus,
personal
perceptions,
belief systems,
cultural factors
and a host of
other things.*

Chapter 0:

Becoming Zero To Impact Millions?

"Baravelli, you've got the brain of a four-year-old boy, and I bet he was glad to get rid of it."
Groucho Marx

"Paradox," according to that oft' quoted Webster guy, is: *a statement that seems contradictory, unbelievable, or absurd but that may actually be true in fact; or something inconsistent with common experience.* Interesting. A long time ago somebody knew that things outside the realm of common experience could actually be true in fact. Even that phrase "true in fact" seems redundant, as if truth could possibly not be factual, or facts could possibly not be true. In fact, is anything absolutely true?

In my years on a spiritual path, I began to learn that *neither truth nor facts can be considered absolute. Both are very much relative to common experience, consensus, personal perceptions, belief systems, cultural factors and a host of other things.* This is often forgotten. So when you don't agree with my

In many ways, man's inhumanity to man can be traced to an incredibly strong desire we all share to be right.

I strive to reconcile the first and foremost paradox in my experience: being less to become more.

How is it that the less I become, the more I influence others?

I spend less time in judging good and bad, and more time in awe.

"truth," that creates an apparent separation between you and I. Since you're obviously wrong, I am therefore justified in my attempts to convince you, to manipulate you, to judge you, to hate you, even to kill you, since I have the truth on my side. In this way, the belief in the absoluteness of truth and facts has indeed led to all kinds of suffering, hatred, and war. *In many ways, man's inhumanity to man can be traced to an incredibly strong desire we all share to be right.*

What if we WERE all right? Or all wrong? Scientists tell us that we are aware of far less than 1% of all the energies bombarding our senses in any moment. From this incredibly narrow perspective, the brain puts together its version of "reality." Having done this, it then vehemently defends its position, using this defense as another bit of evidence of our separation from everyone and everything else. Some of us learn to attack in our defense; others to become so pliant that we agree with everything in order to avoid confrontation (that would include me); while still others simply enjoy arguing. Most of us come from a place of separation and learn strategies to manipulate our worlds as much as possible so they conform to our limited perspectives.

All this judgment and manipulation and limitation keeps us so busy, we don't even realize all the things we're missing. Things like love, joy, peace, abundance, harmony, and wisdom; things that are built into the heart and are extremely difficult to experience when we seek them outside of ourselves.

My goal has been to move from my head to my heart. To open my heart wide and bask in the glow of the glorious gifts contained therein, and to share them with the world. *I strive to reconcile the first and foremost paradox in my experience: being less to become more.* I borrowed this one... When asked if he desired to become the president of India, Mahatma Gandhi replied, "I want to be zero. And I want my actions to affect millions of people." Definitely a paradox there.

How is it that the less I become, the more I influence others? What did Jesus mean when he reminded us that "of himself, he could do nothing?" I think Gandhi and Jesus were talking about the same thing. Of themselves, they could do nothing, and when they removed themselves from the equation, they changed the world.

When I become less, by relegating the *Schmootz Brigade* to lesser status, I allow more of Spirit's perfection in and out. I am closer to True Present Time, and therefore closer to expressing the perfection that I am in essence. My movie is then closer to the Creator's Idea. *I spend less time in judging good and bad, and more time in awe.* I express my gifts and my mission, closer to my maximum potential, and closer to Divine design.

The Innate Intelligence within me, which I refer to as "Innate," not only knows how to run my physiology, performing and coordinating 600,000,000,000,000,000,000,000 things in every second, It knows how to run my life! According to chiropractic philosophy, *Innate is the personification of Universal Intelligence, or God. It is my connection to All. It knows how to run my life from a place of wholeness, love and service, with the biggest of pictures in mind.* I don't know how to do that. I'm generally too busy running away from the present moment to run much of anything.

I believe there's a plan for everything in this Universe, and apparently I'm in it, so that includes me. And you, too. I don't think it's the kind of plan that's etched in stone; but somehow the whole thing is rigged so that everything works. 98% of the atoms that comprise my physical body are replaced in one year. New ones arrive *thru* my consumption of Twinkies, and other than the occasional emergence of a new gray hair, it still

Innate is the personification of Universal Intelligence, or God. It is my connection to All. It knows how to run my life from a place of wholeness, love and service, with the biggest of pictures in mind.

looks like me! Seems like a plan to me! My Innate converts Twinkies into me! It nearly triggers an acid flashback when I really ponder the conspiracy that goes on in our behalf. The intricacy and interconnectedness of the dance in which all of creation is engaged is truly mind-boggling.

Just to consider the workings of my own body or even a single cell in my body is humbling to my puffed-up little mind. That doesn't stop it from thinking it can do better, of course. This is one of the most dangerous hallucinations that brains conjure. Sure, I can't rub my belly and pat my head at the same time, but not only can I do better than this body, I can do better than whatever it is that keeps an entire universe in balance and harmony. Uh-huh. *Only in those decreasingly rare moments when I am able to sit back and relax fully knowing this uni-verse is indeed one song and I am simply an indispensable note, do I become zero—my mind is in time out, and I feel the connection. I feel the plan. And I feel my impact.*

I have experienced this most vividly while doing chiropractic missions in Central America. My wife Hillary, my daughter Ari, and I have participated in six missions: four in Panama, one in Costa Rica, and one in the Dominican Republic.

Since chiropractic is simply removing interference to the expression of the plan in anything with a spine, we delivered that gift to people with whom we couldn't converse, people to whom we couldn't have an attachment, people of whom we couldn't have an expectation, and people from whom we didn't desire to receive anything. Deprived of all that usual brain

Every single piece is part of the big picture, and it definitely fits in somewhere… as more pieces come together, it gets easier to fit new ones in. I rarely look at the pieces of my life that way. I should. I would suffer far less.

food, and not having any time to think anyway, we were forced to open our hearts and deliver our gifts, just for the sake of giving, loving and serving. And the response was enormous every time.

The third time we went to Panama, 147 chiropractors adjusted over 300,000 people in six days. Miracles abounded; people got out of wheel chairs, hearing was restored, the nation's crime rate went down! Many of us had the crystal clear experience of being used by God, undoubtedly because we became zero. We became, as the great Native American, Black Elk, urged us to become, "clean hollow bones" for God to express *thru*. And when that happens, whether in Panama or in our everyday lives, miracles follow. I want more!

It's been gray and rainy in these parts, which in a way has been a nice break from the yards of snow we were getting before winter's official arrival. It's been nice, too, especially as the holiday season has wound down, because it has given us the excuse to stay inside a bit more—it's difficult to *not feel guilty* while ignoring my dog's plaintive face when the sun is shining. We don't get too much of what I call jigsaw puzzle weather.

We've had time to sit with our intentions and goals and promotions for the New Year. We've been playing a lot with one of Ari's holiday gifts—I always get her the stuff I liked when I was a kid! And we're recovering from all that fun and relaxation we just endured in Hawaii. Our trip was perfect. *Thru* the realization it *brot* (no "ughs" this year!) of the importance of friendship, I've been gifted with another wonderful piece.

Do you know what I mean? Lately, life seems to come in pieces, like a jigsaw puzzle. Every experience, every person, every issue, every voice within me, every moment, is a piece. And God has the box with the big picture on it, while all my senses provide are the pieces. From one or two pieces—or two million for that matter—my brain generally thinks it knows the whole picture. I'd do really well on that old TV show "Concentration." In life it doesn't work as well. My assumptions and analyses and judgments are based on far less than the big picture, causing nothing but trouble; and yet on I go thinking I have all the pieces. I don't.

We've done lots of jigsaw puzzles, and I've noticed that some of the pieces invariably end up on the floor or stuck in the corners of the box. Some we never find. Among the ones we do, some are always easy to find and for others we hunt for hours. And some always seem to go directly where they fit, and others we try to

What if our first thot concerning any event is that it is a piece, not good or bad, and that it fits somewhere as part of the perfect whole?

What if we realize we actually created or attracted this very piece in order to realize more of that whole?

What if our every thot and action is toward the whole and not the piece, toward connection and not separation, toward love and not fear?

force into where they don't really go. Some contain clear images of part of the picture, and others appear to contain no new information until they are placed within the framework of others. I never look at a piece of a jigsaw puzzle and throw it away, or bury it, or react emotionally to it, or get attached to it. Sometimes I have to put one aside temporarily and see where it fits later. Yet, I never feel guilty about doing that; nor do I worry about it not fitting. I realize *every single piece is part of the big picture, and it definitely fits in somewhere.* And I also realize *that as more pieces come together, it gets easier to fit new ones in.*

I rarely look at the pieces of my life that way. I should. I would suffer far less.

When I do a jigsaw puzzle, I've found it works best to look at the whole picture first and THEN see how an individual piece fits. Usually in life we create an imaginary big picture from a single piece! That's what these brains do best. Invariably my imaginary big picture is different from yours. How could it not be? Yet, I assume yours should be the same as mine. AND I'll even defend mine, try to get you to change yours, and get pissed off if you don't! I expend loads of energy attempting to manipulate every piece I encounter into my private hallucination. Due to the sheer futility of this endeavor I experience moments of utter despair, raging anger and stark loneliness. Man, I'm nuts.

Does any of this sound familiar to you?

For me, the only answer to this madness is the spiritual life. What would life be like if we considered all its many pieces against a framework of the big picture? The big picture of wholeness and connection and love? The big picture of Innate? Of God? *What if our first thot concerning any event is that it is a piece, not good or bad, and that it fits somewhere as part of the perfect whole?* Beyond that, *what if we realize we actually created or attracted this very piece in order to realize more of that whole? What if our every thot and action is toward the whole and not the piece, toward connection and not separation, toward love and not fear?* One of my teachers used to tell us to "act with love, react with faith." My greatest mentor, Dr. Jim Sigafoose, reminds us to "walk by faith, not by sight." Aren't they saying the same thing?

Does any of this apply to chiropractic?

First of all, what doesn't? Every day in my office, I am confronted with pieces. Symptoms, questions, histories, opinions, personalities, procedures, etc. I was trained to assemble, from this soup of pieces, big pictures called diagnoses and treatment plans and prognoses and reports and the like. Yet, true chiropractic philosophy dictates a more jigsaw puzzle way of looking at things. Start with the big picture (Innate Intelligence as a personification of Universal Intelligence or God) and see where the pieces fit within that framework. It's all perfect. I don't have to change a piece, or fix it, or mask it, I simply have to remove interference to allow that piece to fit more easily and beautifully into the whole.

It requires faith… every time my focus and intent are on the big picture, the world heals.

This is ultimately the purpose of chiropractic, and it gives me countless opportunities to work toward becoming zero. This is harder to do. *It requires faith.* It requires me to forget my programmed tendencies. But *every time my focus and intent are on the big picture, the world heals.* All the pieces simply bring me peace. Peace.

♥   ♥   ♥

ON THE PATH

On the path, I am never alone
My doubts tag along
Old thot patterns cling like burrs
My ego beckons me to turn back

"Things were so nice before," it mutters
"Everyone liked you"
"No rejection; no waves did you make"
"You submitted to all my commands"

So what if my life had no meaning?
No purpose or mission
No message to share with the world
No impact on a blessed soul?

It was comfortable, I recall
To sleep thru life
Floating along in tune with the echoes
Of the world's transient allures

Alas, my eyes have been opened
And it's too late
To ever return to the sleep walk
That was my life as a victim

Ego may sing its sweet lullabies
Or resort to old tricks
Like moaning "who cares"
While it gets me to beat myself up

If I allow this, the suffering mounts
And I fret and whine
Since I ought to know better, and
Awareness becomes the booby prize

But I've learned to jump from the boat
And remember my connection

To Spirit and to all of creation
And rest in the arms of Perfection

When I remember, my vision is clear
The fears subside
The voices dissipate like
morning's mist
Revealing my true and highest path

So thru all the seeming chaos
The roller coaster of thots
The endless detours
and distractions
I serve my mission with joy
and faith

On the path, I am never alone
Innate is with me
And Its love resounds thru
This awesome deal I call my life

On the path,
I am never
alone
Innate is
with me
And Its love
resounds thru
This awesome
deal I call
my life

♥   ♥   ♥

Poetry dwells just below the surface of *thot*, and with our spiritual hammer, ax and pick, perhaps we can unearth a few gems.

Then we can mark them way up above retail while we're raping the earth with our rapacious rapacious-ness, all the while whistling our happy tunes upon the starboard side of the hill, where, of course, the grass is greener and way more expensive. Does it rankle your little nerves to see the plight of indigenous swallows that can never return to San Juan Capistrano without a note from their mothers? Or are you so cold that the mere sight of you could freeze the smile off the Pieta? Whoa there, Millie, don't be blasphemin'; the Lord waits for slip-ups and then sends them to be reupholstered by the genius of fabric himself—Barney Rubble.

I look behind the appearance and there I may find absolutely nothing, Good God y'all, except the truth! And then I have a choice: submit for polygraph analysis or change my thinking.

What evil awaits those that turn their egos to the sun? At the worst, Ego might get a really bad sunburn, and have to wear a T-shirt when it goes swimming. How demeaning! That would really be bad for its ego, for sure, but really good for you and me and for the world! I can slide head first into each moment and if I have to knock the crap out of the fielder at the base, never mind, he's just "pretty and witty and gay."

A committee should be organized to analyze me, and wouldn't that be a kick in the groin for all concerned?

Why do I ever think? It just gets in the way of all this subterranean genius that lies bubbling beneath the surface of my little peewee brain that is otherwise concerned exclusively with eat this and smoke that and I'm right and you're wrong and I'm better than him and she's better than me. What a crock of crock-pots!

To think for one moment
That thinking for one moment
Even begins to compare with
Not thinking in this moment
Is the height of thinking in the
moment, if you ask me—Which
you didn't,
But if you're looking for privacy,
Write your own book.
Leaves leave and senses leave
and folks leave
And we'll leave when we're
damn good & ready—so there.
Rough and ready and all that rot.
Theodore Roosevelt led the
charge,
But James Watt couldn't hold
the charge.
So the rest of us get charged
way more than is allowable
"except void where prohibited
by law."

When in my head, generally, every chance of growth or connection is rained out.

Innate is my third base coach and it waves me home every time. No losses, no shutouts, no putouts, only assists.

Oh well. I'm not sure if that's poetry, but at least it didn't come from my head. *When in my head, generally, every chance of growth or connection is rained out.* We'll play a doubleheader tomorrow and it'll do the same thing.

It's mind-boggling. The mind boggles, it bobbles, it screws up royally, it falls asleep on the job. It creates havoc and pain and suffering, and the insurance companies won't even reimburse you for it. And yet I still tune in to it as if it were God. My-my. No matter how many times I've seen the miracles and the natural rightness of allowing myself to be directed by Innate, the *Schmootz Brigade* still tends to jump in with its tall tales of woe. It slings fastball after fastball of sh-t and often I sit there and take third strikes. But more and more I swing away and sometimes even ignore what's being thrown and simply run around the bases stealing Ego's signals. *Innate is my third base coach and it waves me home every time. No losses, no shutouts, no putouts, only assists.* And I stand in the batter's box of life with my pen and my heart on my sleeve and I easily and effortlessly hit home runs over the walls of illusion and doubt.

My mind really and obviously bugs me sometimes. Why can't it just enjoy each moment? Where is this mechanism that causes it to worry, fret and feel guilty? Where is the switch to turn it off?

The switch is in my heart. It opens and a floodtide of love and awareness calms the surging seas of my mind, like a gentle wind pushing out a storm. The storm always lurks, but it has no power if I don't recognize it. I'm always working to disempower my surging mind, since it is usually dead wrong.

Dead wrong, that's an interesting expression. Well, it's nice to be wrong and alive, and even nicer to be wrong and loving. I can see the need-to-be-right hitchhiking along the byways of my brain that are becoming less and less traveled. I can see it now... pulling up its pant leg in an attempt to look more attractive, continually bypassed by my new choices. It's beautiful out there on those long deserted stretches, and now I can enjoy the scenery, instead of flowing rapidly down the stream in my dream without even the awareness to scream. Ice cream, get your tootsie-frootsie! Get your tootsies off the couch! Don't you know company is coming and the plastic has to look transparent so we can pretend it's not there despite the obvious sensation of melting plastic you feel under your behind? Dead wrong.

Yes, indeed, now I'm watching ever attentively. And I forgive myself. Disempowerment is not where it's at. Where it's at is on the inside: the core—my heart. Innate sings *thru* it like one of those old megaphones. And that song echoes *thru* the recesses of time and space, reverberating in each cell and in each atom of my being, and then out into the ethers to the realm of All. All was never our favorite detergent, but All is all there is, if you catch my drift (otherwise I'd be worried about you). I feel Innate rising up. It's coming like the cavalry without the drama and the bugles. And hopefully, without John Wayne, too.

Maybe I'm doing all right. I give myself an A-minus and my ego an Incomplete for being so incomplete in its awareness of the big picture. Ego, you are a classic underachiever and a major source of disappointment. "Dis" appointment just for you or for your entire family? How does 3:00 on Friday work for you?

Yes, I am doing all right, in my humble opinion, and part of that all-right-ness is that I consider my opinion to be humble. Dr. Stew, it is our humble opinion that you've done a good job with your life. We're happy with you, happy for you, and happy being you. Thank you, Stew. Thank you, Innate, and thank you, God, for creating Stew and allowing him to grow and develop and co-create—and procreate for that matter (we can't forget that one now, can we?).

Life is wonderful. I float on wings of truth and connection, merrily reminding myself that life is but a dream, and yet while I stay awake it has a very real impact on all. All's well that ends well? Nah, all's well, period. It doesn't end. It just flows, directionless and forever, onward and upward and downward and backward, in and *thru*, around, everywhere and always.

♥   ♥   ♥

I've known some people who were heavily into

*Whenever
I give my power
away to outside
influences,
especially when
I play the victim
of those
influences,
I lose some of
the true Power
that Innate
provides to
manifest the life
of my dreams.*

astrology. That worked for them, of course; but you could never count on them for anything when Mercury was in retrograde motion.

Somehow, I hate the idea of being controlled by distant rocks, as if I was a puppet on a string. I certainly acknowledge the fact that we are subject to many energies and influences from the outside. And yet every Twinkie atom in my body resonates with the belief that we are one with the Creator, and therefore, limitlessly able to exert tremendous power in our lives based on our energy, our intent, our focus, and our love. It's an inside job!

Another paradox goes whizzing around my cortical neurons like a really nauseating roller coaster. Invariably it ends up at the same place: *whenever I give my power away to outside influences, especially when I play the victim of those influences, I lose some of the true Power that Innate provides to manifest the life of my dreams.* Since I can only control what goes out from my consciousness, I am always better served, as is the world, by maintaining my focus on that.

There are countless opportunities to feel powerless. A one half-hour news broadcast contains many. Politics always makes me feel hopeless and manipulated. News in my own profession often provides the same opportunities. What can I do? I deeply appreciate the warriors we have, both in the principled chiropractic political arena as well as in the environmental and peace arenas, and I will write letters until my fingers ache; but politics is not going to be my real contribution, that much I know. What then?

My brain hasn't been very helpful with its tendency to come from a place of separation and powerlessness. It bounces back and forth between denial and anger, between resignation and revenge; what can I change on the outside? Innate, speaking *thru* my heart as always, thankfully reminds me to look within and to stay in my power. "Worried about medical ideas taking over the chiropractic profession?" It asks, "Well then, how free of medical ideas is your own consciousness?" Hmmm. While I'm at it, how free of hate and greed and everything else I don't like in the world is my consciousness?

Last week I attended a memorial service for one of our practice folks who died ten days ago with metastatic liver cancer, at age 49. I'd been adjusting her for about six weeks. Cynthia was only the second adult in my care under the age of eighty-something to die on me in sixteen years. Both had cancer. Both waited too long to come in. Both received a ton of hope thru the chiropractic principle. Both did extremely well under care. Both tried really hard to have faith, only to lose it because of symptoms and pronouncements from the "experts." I adjusted Cynthia to turn on the power; I loved her; I saw her whole and healed and perfect. I knew without a glimmer of doubt that she would heal. And last week I listened to dozens of her friends and family beautifully recounting stories of the wonderful, giving person Cynthia was.

As I listened, *thots* of powerlessness tried to creep in. Not so much involving my inability to keep her alive, but more about my inability to prevent her from giving away her own power. Cynthia gave to many causes and to many people her whole life, but did she ever truly learn to receive? In the end, did she fully accept her healing? Did she fully accept God's love? Or was she literally tapped out? *Now* she is healed, and *now* she is basking in God's love. I wish I could have helped her realize these things while she was still here in her body, but as always, I don't know the plan. And I knew as I sat and listened, it is infinitely more productive to consider these lessons for myself.

How much power have I stolen from practice folks over the years

How much of my own power have I given away forgetting the Source of everything in my own life?

having them look to me as the one doing the healing? *How much of my own power have I given away forgetting the Source of everything in my own life?*

Gandhi told us, "You must be the change you wish to see in the world." He didn't say we had to buy the change, or figure it out, or wait for others to do it, or to complain about it not happening. He said we had to be the change first. And as we work toward becoming zero, the changes we bring about in the world are infinitely loving and abundant. That is the gift he *brot* to the world, as did Jesus, Buddha, Martin Luther King, and many others. But I'm concerned that the world can't wait for another "savior" to happen along. You and I must be the change.

So, what is the point of all this rambling? Who knows? For me, it is a clear reminder of where my true Power comes from, and of the consequences of looking elsewhere. My senses bombard me with seemingly bad news, the world seems clueless and careening toward destruction, and chiropractic continues to circle the wagons and shoot inward. And I can't help thinking it's all for the same reason. We've forgotten where the Power is. In my own profession, we talk about the Power a lot, and we forget it a lot. In and out of chiropractic, we're all in the world, and I suppose we must play in the political arena.

And what would happen if we all remembered the Power in every moment? What would happen if we all became clear conduits for that Power? What would happen if, during every interaction we ever had with anyone, we tapped into that Power, acknowledged It in us and them, told the truth, and then, in a state of total presence and connection, simply loved? What would happen if we truly and completely became maximum expressions of Innate? Would the world change? When will it change? Are we all waiting for a political solution, or for Mercury to come out of retrograde?

♥　　♥　　♥

September 11th, 2002

Every time we connect with that Innate place within us, peace is created in the world.

Beloved Creator,
As you know, 46 years ago today I was born into this world. Thank you for that! And as you know, too, this world has seen its share of hate and violence and war and greed and poverty and disease. For millennia, we as humans have begged, pleaded, whined, and bargained with you to erase these things. A quick look around, however, indicates clearly that we still have them all.

Some say that is evidence you do not exist, or do not care, or are somehow vengeful. I say we have been in error expecting you to work miracles upon us, when you are constantly and tirelessly working miracles thru us.

Today, I simply ask you to help us remember that you have lovingly placed peace, love, brotherhood, abundance, and health right inside each and every one of us. These are your thots, and I ask that you help us become zero so we can hear them and live them. We are all instruments of your peace.

Every time we connect with that Innate place within us, peace is created in the world. Thank you for that place, and for our intention to take up residence in that place. And thank you for the gifts you have given me that allow others to find that same place.

Your child,
Stew

♥   ♥   ♥

Chapter 1:

Discipline Leads To Freedom?

Anatomy Professor:
"This is the liver."
Groucho: *"What, no bacon?*
I'd send that back if I were you."

Yes, this dedicated follower of fashion has returned to writing after a long hiatus. Ah, discipline. Preferring to write longhand as I do—I still haven't gotten fast enough in the typing department to keep up with my first *thots*—my shoulder has limited my participation in writing ventures for the past few months. It still hurts a bit now. Trying to find a comfortable position is difficult, so try to catch these words as I float the book around under my hand.

Life is grand, strike up the band; the staccato drumbeat of my heart is stirring the ashes of principle and inspiration around the world! I've just done five talks in the last five days, and I am pleased to report that I can assess my abilities as a speaker without too much giggling or nausea. In fact, I am getting good, just like I never knew I would. Mostly well received, perhaps somewhat admired? *Thot* of as crazy? It's amazing how the same words can elicit so many different feelings and responses.

Hold on a moment as I move the book and sip some coffee, as discipline again and again rears its lovely head above the shrouded mists of Ego's sensation-based addictions.

Oh little coffee mug, I see you standing alone, without a love of your own, yet looking so attractive there on my left. My left-hand man, you might say. On we go to better things, as I've found myself Innate's wings. To Pretoria we march, on a treadmill called time, whistling Dixie *thru* our apertures of hope.

Speaking of speaking, my voice gets hoarse from the screaming I tend to do, and that (as well as my shoulder) reminds me *this is God's voice, pen and hands, heart and soul here, so I'd better take better care of them all.* Got to keep them ringing and singing to their highest frequency, their highest vibration. Working on keeping in cycle with

This is God's voice, pen and hands, heart and soul here, so I'd better take better care of them all.

Discipline leads to freedom, even tho that never used to make sense to me at all.

Be a disciple to Innate, so discipline can come easily and naturally.

the flow of all perfection, I do occasionally overindulge in things that are best kept to a level of mild moderation. Things that are blissfully wonderful in their occasional-ness.

Yes, *discipline leads to freedom, even tho that never used to make sense to me at all*. Discipline is essential in my quest of becoming a clean, hollow bone.

The point is, I am emerging from long standing *thots* of self-sabotage. And camouflage—that word didn't really apply, but I just wanted to prove to my fifth grade teacher that I could spell it, as *that* was the word that cost me the fifth grade spelling bee championship.

Am I forever doomed to give away my gifts with pain? Adjusting and writing hurt my shoulder and speaking hurts my voice and pocket book.

Ah, why whine about such small matters? They are all simply loving reminders of my peewee thinking and my ego's conspiracy to keep me extremely weak, small and undisciplined while it frolics with bullsh-t about my wonderful-osity. Perhaps as long as it really doesn't hurt me or anyone else, it's OK to pamper and enjoy myself once in a while? I can even occasionally pamper the *Schmootz Brigade!* Indeed, it deserves a reward for not following the same old Mississippi Rivers in my brain, and for taking a back seat without *too much* back seat driving. *That* must be hard for a chauffeur—to suddenly sit well behaved in the back and not even offer suggestions or directions unless the car is really threatened. So I can love the *Schmootz Brigade* and be gentle with its fits of insanity.

Nay, *tho* I dance *thru* the valley of the shadow of Ego, I will fear no bullsh-t. I will jump out of the boat

It's only hard when I'm thinking about me. From a place of connection there can be no lack of discipline, no ugliness, no lack, no impatience, no time, space, evil, disease, bad, whatever. There can be no paradox, only perfection.

Today I will partake totally in this world, enjoying and participating in each blessed, sacred moment, watching from my beautiful spot outside the world—here in my heart.

and observe from my grassy hillock of love. I better not pout just because Ego is going to town. Santa Claus is coming to take its place, and it is a sure-fire thing he knows I've been naughty but oh so nice. Otherwise the Laplander can land in someone else's lap for a change. For I am a peak eagle of love, a principled expression of Life, a master of communicating the good news of natural wonder and perfection, streaming *thru* the years in this earth-suit toward greater and greater awareness and truth.

So there, Shoulder. I feel you tugging at my greatness and power. Just for that, I won't even let you read the book when it's done.

Hello Hillary, you skinny sexy wonderful complex simple childlike tyrannical loving hating beautiful agonizing soul mate! You mirror my beauty as well as my grotesque, evil, silly, stupid separateness. But I am learning to see the beauty even *thru* the gargoyle—in you, and especially in me. I stay connected—that's it! Stay connected to what I AM. The whole thing is so easy. *Be a disciple to Innate, so discipline can come easily and naturally.* Why is it so hard?

It's only hard when I'm thinking about me. From a place of connection there can be no lack of discipline, no ugliness, no lack, no impatience, no time, space, evil, disease, bad, whatever. There can be no paradox, only perfection. I do feel and remember that perfection and it always dances and floats, even if sometimes it seems just outside my grasp. Well, on with the day.

Today I will partake totally in this world, enjoying and participating in each blessed, sacred moment, watching from my beautiful spot outside the world— here in my heart. Here also, in our lovely home and our fabulous practice at magnificent Lake Tahoe. So love it all! Work it, let it go, work it, let it go... Put energy into it because we love it, like a plant or a bird or a dog that we treasure. Or a child. Love it; nurture it; watch it grow; watch its cycles; let it go.

Life. Practice. Child-raising. Relationship. Life. All the same. Let it go; let it flow. Put some action in and love it, and don't get involved with how much or when or even why. Let's get involved in each moment, for in each moment lies the sum total of every conceivable triumph, every conceivable happiness, and every conceivable loving experience.

♥   ♥   ♥

The years go by in this free willed, predestined paradox of spiritual reality called life. Or you could call it Ray. If I have created all this; if this is all the objectified substance of my consciousness; if this is all a movie that Innate projects onto the perceptual screen of my senses, then let there be light! Let there be clarity, energy, focus, and above all else, love and fun. OK, I am in this body. Or am I? I am seemingly in this body because my mind believes it. Or *maybe I have a mind and a body because I believe those things are necessary in order to learn the things I need to learn?* Or maybe I just choose to believe I have this mind and body so I can be so completely entertained by the twisted turns these *thots* take *thru* the experiences of perception and of sensation that provide all the drama in my life. Maybe I just think I'll be bored, and so I choose this eventful, illusory existence, inviting all sorts of things in from the outside. Things outside do not create happiness, but they can add to the fullness of my being. They can contribute to the full spectrum of experience and alter my perceptions.

Still, I choose to explore the true happiness of my Self. Within— that's where I want to rest, whether

> *Maybe I have a mind and a body because I believe those things are necessary in order to learn the things I need to learn?*

I find it boring or not. Only *thots* of boredom create boredom. The sky and sea are never boring, always changing, always perfect, always beautiful. And therefore, so am I. I am that. Never boring, always creating. So let's see where this magnificent brain can take us. Let's see what this incredible receiving device for God can pick up…

The ides of May are upon us, and the eyes of Texas are upon us, and upon us come the Knights of Pythias, blazing a torrid trail across the deep blue terrain without a paddle. "Nevermore" quoth the raven with a lithp. The speech therapist was arrested for practicing Perquacky without a license and will now and forever be referred to as "a quack." There you have it, folks, the latest rundown and lowdown on the goose down quilts that are now down so low you have to crawl into the bargain basement to find them. Undoubtedly my mind is reeling and never feeling because the ceiling of its outlook is unbelievably lowdown. Where oh where has my little mind gone? Oh where oh where can it be? It has lost its sheep to Little Bo Peep and I hear she's keeping it in a jar with Miss Muffet's curds and whey—what a way to go! My, this particular paragraph is clearly infected with conjecture; so take it and ponder its significance until the cows come home, wagging my mind behind them.

But wait! There's more. Saint Nick isn't ready for Easter because too many eggs spoil the broth, and nobody really likes broth anyway unless they're sick. You'd have to be sick. Life is

All of a sudden, I found myself focusing on things I thot I had pretty much let go of. Things like jealousy, judgment and lack.

wonderful, and the heat is on, boy. But it's nice and cool and calm and collected here on Innate's bosom where I will continue to lay my head. Tom Dooley ought to know better, but I don't think anyone told him about the price of laying one's head anywhere else. Go ahead, Tom, and bring Bill Bailey home while you're at it.

Seriously, folks, life is truly terrific, and Manifestation has been on the menu ever since the new chef arrived, Awareness Johnson. Instant manifestation. But no one is complaining because in this case, it's a lot better than Potato Buds or Folgers Crystals—even if it can't be served in some of America's finest restaurants. It can, however, be found in fine boutiques wherever lip guards are sold. Guard your lip and guard your heart and never the twain shall meet. Twain did live nearby but everyone was so confused about what his real name was they're still banning his books today. Pretty serious, huh?

Well, we plod on, stumbling like old drinking buddies —Innate, Ego, and me. I'm getting there without any idea where "there" is. But "here" feels pretty good. So I know that as I get there, it will still be here—and that's not hearsay. So there! You can't call that boring!

♥   ♥   ♥

Smack dab in the middle of the second day of "poor me," I take to pen because for me, clarity often follows writing like a dutiful hound.

Things have been so incredibly wonderful, and I have been feeling very much focused on and connected to Innate, while being very much aware of the often instantaneous and bountiful manifestation of all my desires. Opportunities have arisen in abundance at every turn. Events follow a clear rhythm of synchronicity. People I have needed to connect with appear magically. Blessings and gifts have rained on me in a deluge. I have found myself literally daily, sharing a private chuckle with myself, amused over the repetitive *thot, "Wow,* didn't THAT work out perfectly?"

A few days ago, for instance, I learned that the cruise ship which my family rescheduled for later in the year had a "minor mishap" at sea. At least three people sustained broken bones and many more had the poop scared out of them. *That* is just the latest example of the *perfect flow* in my life.

So, what happened yesterday?

All of a sudden, I found myself focusing on things I thot I had pretty much let go of. Things like jealousy, judgment and lack. And this was going on while I was adjusting! It has become so rare to be anything but totally focused and connected in the office that at first I was unsure what was happening. When I heard myself asking, "Where the heck is so and so?" and barking at family and staff like a frightened mongrel, I started to get the idea. So I remembered my discipline and used my tools: I directed the luminescent beam of my presence and awareness on these disruptive *thots*. They very calmly put on their sunglasses. I loved them and blessed them—they really liked that. I laughed at them. They laughed right back. *I did my Chi Gung exercise specifically for getting rid of bad chi. They simply laughed at me in Chinese.* I replaced them with *thots* of gratitude, connection, abundance, and Spirit. As soon as my back was turned, they gleefully stole the spotlight once again. I surrendered, and they've been waltzing across the dance floor of my consciousness ever since.

Two bits of what seems like good news just occurred to me.

One is: *thru* this whole thing I

I did my Chi Gung exercise specifically for getting rid of bad chi. They simply laughed at me in Chinese.

(Innate) have been Watching, Observing, Noticing. Feeling, and in so doing, I discovered how much my mind still limits me. What nerve! I created the damned thing! Its physical nature and its *thots* are made up of My Divine Substance, and all it wants to do is screw me up.

Here I am continually pouring out My Essence of love and service to this body, this mind, and all creation, and the best my mind can come up with is, "Where's so and so?" Yapping, whining, groaning, and sucking its thumb? Yep, full of sh-t, all right.

Even while I focused on feeling the stuck energy inside of me, intending to simply *be* with it and let it go, my mind has cut in on my attention like an overeager suitor at a dance, wanting to characterize and label the feeling. Well, my little demon mind, you are nuts, yet, I know deep in my Being that as I continue to watch you, you will shape up. And in the meantime, I must admit, you serve me rather well on occasion.

Which brings me to the second bit of good news. In the book *Das Energi*, by Paul Williams, he says something to the effect of, "To go 95% of the way is to suffer total insanity; to go *all the way* is to be free." I can relate. This has seemed like insanity. I realized at times over the past two days that I was just being tested, and my mind clung to its mantra: "I don't need this test anymore." I guess it was wrong. For now I see very clearly that I have not gone all the way. I am not yet free. And this insanity is as perfect as everything else has been. It is Ego-mind's last stand—hopefully! A desperate attempt to get me to continue to identify with it. That's why it has gone such lengths to get me

I feel another layer has been peeled, another mask discarded. How many more remain is a mystery.

I am left with gratitude for my process, gratitude for my discipline, gratitude for my mission, gratitude for all my fellow servants of that mission, and mostly, gratitude for the perfection that is. And for the Source of it.

to figure all this out. "Maybe," it dreams, "if I figure this out for him, he'll let me back on center stage. Maybe if I keep him busy with my yarns of separation he'll forget everything he's learned." I realize now, I have been observing and noticing my *thots* with my mind; I have been judging them from a place that I *thot* was me, but was merely a different facade.

What I didn't do was accept my *thots* as perfect. Perfect because they clearly point out the cracks in my sacred container; perfect because they clearly show me the piles of excrement that they manifest; perfect because they are born from Perfection. Certainly no less perfect than all the "good" stuff that has shown up in my life lately. Maybe I'll never get *all the way* there, but the next time I am in this place, I will not judge it as anything other than perfect.

Well, I'm not sure if you would call all that clarity, but I sure feel a lot better. *I feel another layer has been peeled, another mask discarded. How many more remain is a mystery.* And all this has been a further unfolding of the Great Mystery. *I am left with gratitude for my process, gratitude for my discipline, gratitude for my mission, gratitude for all my fellow servants of that mission, and mostly, gratitude for the perfection that is. And for the Source of it.* On to the next layer!

♥   ♥   ♥

I read somewhere that Gandhi had a greedy nature and he used it to further his mission of peace. That's what I'd like to do. I can chain the *Schmootz Brigade* to the wheels of the juggernaut that is my life and let them row for a while. They can help steer me toward what I want, while I mentally put them in the back seat.

Well, OK, you can drive for a bit, guys, but you must understand that when we get there—wherever that might be—you'll have to pay full price like everyone else. And as we go on you will have to accept more meaningless jobs that don't involve management. You can be independent contractors that provide a little incentive for me, but under no circumstances can you veto any decisions of the Board. And please be diligent in limiting your comments to one per hour. Maybe that way we can get something done around here. So, *Schmootz Brigade*, you are hereby informed that things are going to be different and I think it's time you gave up your key to the executive washroom. I think we're absolutely and completely capable of running the show, considering the Main Man runs the whole universe without a shred of assistance from you. So there.

I realize that the *Doodoo Brigade* does motivate me

to share my gifts with the world, even if it does so for its own personal aggrandizement. Like Gandhi's greediness, at least that helps me to fulfill my mission, and I'm grateful for that. And I do have a request, oh mighty legion of feces. Can you help with a little incentive toward this physical discipline thing?

What a remarkable machine this body is. All the little workers constantly cleaning up, repairing; nonstop maintenance crews scurrying around under the direction of the man upstairs, Innate. An awesome spectacle of healing and wholeness, "Coming soon to a theatre near you. Innate and the Great Cleanse! Starring Peter Prostate in a shrinking role. Claude Colon getting rave reviews for his gut wrenching performance. Harry Heart uttering that classic line, 'Crapola, we don't need no stinking crapola.' With a cast of trillions!" All directed by the greatest of directors, who doesn't even care about getting any billing. It just wants the thing to be harmonious.

A hemorrhoid is scratching at the walls of my rectum saying,

What a remarkable machine this body is. All the little workers constantly cleaning up, repairing; nonstop maintenance crews scurrying around under the direction of the man upstairs, Innate.

"Go ahead; drink that coffee." Are you happy down there, little *hemi*? Are you glad to make me itch? Do you gleefully sit there, puffing out your chest and the walls of my veins, taking pride at the lack of circulation *thru* my liver? Kind of afraid of going *thru* that liver, aren't you? There's some mighty nasty machinery up there. *Those* cells are just plain mean, doncha know. You just stay right there in the warm recesses of my distal colon, and every now and then take in the view over the hilltops of the incredible world outside. Sunshine and even rain and snow occasionally, but I imagine most of the time it just looks like underwear to you. So now I'm writing to my hemorrhoid. Preparation H-101 with a minor in English Literature. Very minor.

The old body is still not 100% in terms of energy, but I can feel it coming. Perhaps a long, lovely walk to the river is in order? To commune with Nature and take her for a chaperoned stroll along the beeches and stately elms... must be someone else's life I'm imagining since we don't have any of those around here. Then to ask her counsel on matters of the heart —she being such an acclaimed advise columnist— and listen as she whispers her sweet mysteries of being, and hums her melodies of manifestation. To feel her stirring with her cycles and her plans for the next creation. Oh, to see her unfold her designs and her whims to this plane of reality, for my mind to see the possibilities of unattached and unconditional love and creation. To taste of her breast, to sample her sweet delights...

I do love Nature and her many faces and moods.

Let me not remain a disciple to my senses, but see, hear, feel, taste and smell everything as a gift from God.

I realize the senses are the portals for the Schmootz Brigade, I love them, as Gandhi undoubtedly loved his greediness, and I allow them to lead me further on this path of freedom, wholeness, service and love.

She is much like Hillary. Both so beautiful, so powerful, so sweet and soft, so creative, so magnificently passionate in their creating, so moody, so bitter at times, so healing and helpful and bitchy. I love them both so. And I love their calming presence, and their continuous acceptance of my attention. Always available for communing.

Yesterday we went to Monitor Pass and saw the trees changing into their yellow/ orange serapes, dancing in the breezes. *Hola.* We sat in the hollowed out cirque of river canyon along the East Fork of the Carson River, and allowed nature to drown out our negativity with her love and power. Such a treat for the senses.

Senses can be such a blessing. Tasting and Smelling are cruder and older yet very emotionally stirring. Hearing is newer — it stands for soundless echoes in the mist. Seeing is the newest — it dominates like Roger Clemens on a good night. And Feeling underlies them all — the most basic caress of the Mother — the one I might miss the most. But cancel that because I prefer to not miss any of them, and instead always be aware of the essence behind and beyond all the physical senses. *Let me not remain a disciple to my senses, but see, hear, feel, taste and smell everything as a gift from God.*

I'm sensing the ability to sense as well as the ability to discriminate what I'm labeling *thru* the senses. Does that make any sense? *I realize the senses are the portals for the Schmootz Brigade, I love them, as Gandhi undoubtedly loved his greediness, and I allow them to lead me further on this path of freedom, wholeness, service and love.*

♥   ♥   ♥

Chapter 2:

Here or There?

"Are you going my way?
Well, you go Uruguay, and I'll go mine."
Groucho Marx

Yesterday was a lovely, cold but clearer than predicted day after waking to a dusting of snow. We had a potluck in the office and it was sparsely attended but nice. I did everything but actually announce that I wanted to leave town—or did I? Who knows? The food was good, anyway, even if the portions were large. The restaurant business doesn't interest me in the slightest, but then again, why would it?

What business does interest me? None, really. What interests me? Everything, until it becomes a business. I'm not sure this is any business of yours, but I ask you, does this seem like burnout? Is burnout dependent on results? Is it burnout when you love almost every minute that you're doing what it is you're supposedly burnt out on? Hmmm. Doesn't seem likely. What's more likely is that I love being a

I step out of myself… and to hell with the proper dance steps!

*Does anyone have all this stuff figured out?
If so, I'm sure they're wrong.*

*Perfection is just around the corner but life is a circle.
No wonder we're so dizzy.*

chiropractor. I love adjusting the folks. I love turning on the power of life. I love sharing the good news of a life run by Innate. I love what I love, but perhaps there is more I can do?

I'm a blithering idiot but people seem to like what I have to say and write. Go figure. So I will continue to moon walk into the big time, while I step out of myself. I step out with boldness and bigness. Steppin' out with my baa-by. *I step out of myself… and to hell with the proper dance steps!* I make them up as I go along—and the beds, too. Would you like your bed turned down this evening, sir? Or an apple turnover? Or would you like to turn over a new leaf? Sounds good to me. I am going into big time bigness. Will you join me? Even *tho* for the first time in my life I'm not coming apart?

I really am a pip. Gladys Knight would love me, even if my mind is leaving on a midnight train to Georgia.

Does anyone have all this stuff figured out? If so, I'm sure they're wrong.

Well, when all else fails, you

can always take the class over again. And this time don't forget that even *tho* the Gross National Product is grossly unproductive, doesn't it strike you as odd that the sun shines bright on my Old Kentucky Home but Nellie has to wait for it? And while we're on the subject of lamb chops, do you think Shari Lewis ever met Gary Lewis? Or any of the Playboys? Was she ever *in Playboy?* Or would that have been politically incorrect for the rest of the ventriloquists who were not so amply endowed by their Creator with certain inalienable rights? You know, like life, liberty, equality, fraternity, sororities and movies like "Animal House"? I leave it to you.

Do you really intend selling that Volkswagen Bus for 23 cents knowing there are people in China starving for Grateful Dead stickers? In the name of Famous Amos, can you in all good conscience have such a good conscience? Or are you simply farting in the breeze thinking that the world stinks? Do we all continue on, or wear gasmasks?

You know, when you don't think about it, life is pretty darned wonderful. Too late—you *thot* about it already, didn't you? Yes, *perfection is just around the corner, but life is a circle. No wonder we're so dizzy.*

It's July 4th and there aren't too many other holidays left that we actually celebrate on the right day. Happy birthday, America! You're probably wallowing away pulling out 227 birthday candles, drinking beer and watching fireworks, as well as your wallets for another year. Well, this young American is seriously considering heading off to the land from which you fought to gain independence.

Yes, jolly auld England. Sitting there across the sea like an emerald, waiting with open arms and legs for us to come over and change the world, long a British tradition. Sure, you have your own problems but opportunity is knocking and I have a lot of points. Ari, of course, is not thrilled with the idea. Uprooting her would be as hard on her as on all of us; but a strong voice within me is crying out "who cares," because this is starting to feel more and more right. Some strong sense of connection and of being led, pulled, chided and guided, twisted and rocked onto a certain path. A path not of least resistance, but of most insistence. We've asked to serve and this is a golden opportunity. Ah, sweet mystery of life I'm not sure if I've found you. But perhaps another piece? Do I step up to the plate in England with the bases loaded and everyone counting on me to help save chiropractic in Europe? Ego says they've seen me over there and they love

What is a midlife crisis anyway, but taking stock and seeing unfulfilled dreams or areas that can be greater?

me. Well, they do here in my practice, too. I don't know. Clarity is elusive. In the meantime this exciting possibility of extreme change is lurking behind each moment like a pickpocket who wants to be noticed and caught.

Here or there?

Isn't it amazing how many things can be on your mind, and how long they can sit there stewing, brewing, chewing, fermenting and fomenting so much discourse and disgust? My head is perfectly capable of batting this thing around forever. A nonstop never-ending Frisbee game between Ego Left and Ego Right, with nothing gained—but certainly lots to lose. Well, do I want to be caught? I don't remember. What was the question again? It doesn't matter. Should I be worried about all this talking I do with myself? Who am I talking to? There's no one there but little old me and little old me and little old me. All these little old me(s) in here, like an old folks home for Lilliputians. The coast is clear and the fog is lifting and the horizon is looming and the tea is ready and the crumpets are like meaty English muffins—and that's all right, mama!

Maybe this is a mid-life crisis thing. *What is a midlife crisis anyway, but taking stock and seeing unfulfilled dreams or areas that can be greater?* It's not like I want a young blonde or a sports car for chris'sake. I just want to make a difference. I just want to step up and deliver my gifts *without* a delivery charge. And I am ready. Do I step off this ground that is sacred yet somewhat too familiar and stale, and enter the rarified air of the unknown?

♥   ♥   ♥

A decision is made, and widely and dramatically announced in a letter to the chiropractic world:

It is almost exactly 15 years since the State of California, in their infinite wisdom, bestowed upon me a license to practice chiropractic. Little did I know at the time of the enormity of change and growth that event would initiate. Having no grand visions at first, and being basically unconscious, I stumbled blindly thru the highways and byways of things chiropractic. Along the way, I found some success. I discovered some gifts I never knew I possessed. I discovered a love for speaking and writing, and made some impact on the lives of some people, both in my practice and in our profession.

I learned some things about the world and about myself and now feel I know much less than I did back then—which pleases me greatly. And most importantly, because I opened up to Spirit, I have embraced the Great Mystery. I have come to a point where I allow Spirit to work thru me a

I learned some things about the world and about myself and now feel I know much less than I did back then—which pleases me greatly. And most importantly, because I opened up to Spirit, I have embraced the Great Mystery.

good percentage of the time, to speak thru me, to guide me, and to provide for me, in every area of my life. As a result, my life has become a blessed dance of balance, of fulfillment, of joy, of gratitude and of love. And I have asked to serve, to surrender, even more.

Well, I have been reminded once again, rather forcefully, of the old cliché, "be careful what you ask for."

I am standing at the crossroads of a very exciting and immensely scary fork in the road. One possibility is to continue on, straight ahead in the direction I have been traveling where the view is familiar, somewhat comfortable, and apparently safe. Along this road there are signposts that alert me to familiar dangers as well as to new opportunities. This road has brought me much happiness, and my brain is totally convinced this is the only logical path to follow.

The other fork heads toward uncharted territory, so foggy and hazy that I can't see for any distance at all in that direction. This road would be a leap of faith. Following it would mean giving up nearly every loved one and every material "reality" in my life. The dangers and the rewards are totally unknown. At one time in my life, this would have been a ridiculously easy decision. Now, however, my heart is so full of longing for the second fork, and the Winds of Spirit seem to be pushing me so strongly in that direction, that the choice is perhaps the toughest I've been asked to make. And I have made my choice, as some of you already know.

With Hillary and Ari, who have been amazingly supportive of all this, I am leaving my practice, leaving my home of 22 years, leaving my life as I've known it, leaving my parents and family and my dearest friends, and I am following my dream. This may happen in the next few months.

Prior to September 2000, I had never been to Europe. I have now been there three times. After the first trip, I noticed something different upon my return. Every time I traveled previously, regardless of how wonderful or beautiful or life changing the place or experience had been, it was always easy to return to Lake Tahoe and to my life and practice. I was always eager to return to my practice folks, to my totally fulfilling and balanced life, and to the most beautiful place in the world. After the first trip to Europe, some of those usual feelings were missing. It felt like I'd left small pieces of my heart scattered around England and Ireland. Within a short period of time, those pieces seemed to return —around the same time as the post cards we sent—and life was magical again.

The same thing happened, to a somewhat lesser degree, after our trip to France in March. It has been almost six weeks since returning from England again, and the knowing in my heart that I am meant to be there and to serve there has not even remotely left me. If anything, it gets stronger every day.

The chiropractic situation in the UK is also at a crossroads. The government has taken over the profession, and all the chiropractors had to register with the agency in charge. The "powers that be" in the profession over there are, as they seem to be here as well, the medically minded, low back pain types. There is great fear that principled chiropractic will be overrun, that the government will put severe restrictions on chiropractic utilization, and that chiropractic as we know and love it will be swallowed up and absorbed into the vast medical machine.

The rest of Europe seems poised to follow whatever happens in the UK.

There is a tremendous need for chiropractors who can communicate the philosophy and stand with the principled chiropractors over there: to speak the truth; to inspire; to motivate; to teach; to share. Tho my mind constantly questions whether I have the qualifications for the job, my heart tells me to go for it. It is an opportunity for me to really step into my power, to fully use the gifts that I have been given—to serve. I asked to serve, I asked to enlarge my territory of service to God, and I have faith that God's hand will be with me, because I will surely need it!

Thru all this, I am gifted with a further lesson. Since I made my choice, things have been a bit tough. To be OK with my choice, my mind felt the necessity to make everything here "wrong" or "bad" in some way. Just one of the insane games it likes to play. For the first time in many years, I found myself at my office but not there. Not even wanting to be there! It was frightening. It was as if I jumped into the abyss, floating between here and there. Limbo. I had extreme difficulty being in the moment, focusing on where I was and on what I was supposed to be doing to serve here. My mind resorted to more old habits: to force things, to press issues, to plan, to doubt, to worry, to whine, drool and spit. Obstacles suddenly reared their seemingly ugly heads at every turn.

"God, I thot this is what you wanted me to do!" I cried. "Why are you making it so difficult all of a sudden?"

My answer finally came. "When did you decide to take over?"

Hmmm. Yes, I had forgotten how small a role I had played in matters to that point, and how divinely guided it all had been. Things were going magnificently well before I had gotten involved. So I again surrendered.

My focus has been back where it belongs, here and now. And just as suddenly a series of synchronistic and miraculous things have happened to confirm my choice. I realized that it was my willingness to surrender in service and to open myself up these past years that has helped manifest the opportunities I now enjoy. The love for what I do brot me to the brink of a new and exciting chance to expand that love across the "pond."

You who have supported me, and taught me, and loved me, and lifted me, and challenged me, and grown along with me—my fellow warriors and friends, angels and loved ones on this incredible adventure—I thank you! This would have never happened without you. I ask for your prayers as we follow our hearts. A part of me hopes it inspires others to follow theirs. By this magical email phenomenon, I will stay in touch. I will certainly let you know when and where we are going as soon as we find out, and I hope to hear from you. The days ahead will undoubtedly bring chal-lenges, and knowing the immensity of passion and purpose that each of you brings to the world will help us immeasurably.

I truly, honestly, love you all.
Stew

One week later, a second letter is sent:
A funny thing happened on my way to England. I hadn't counted on the Alex factor. As soon as I made the commitment to go, the Universe, as expected, ran a series of obstacles across our path—almost too numerous and mostly too unimportant to mention.

*So much for
expectations.*

*Fifteen years of
practice passed
before my eyes.
The babies,
the hugs,
the healings,
the love;
I laughingly
reflected on
how attached
I still was.*

*I had been
seeing only two
possible paths:
my practice
or my dream.*

We couldn't bring in our pets without putting them in six months of quarantine, for example. No big deal, we'll just go to Spain for seven months and enter the UK from there. Not really what we wanted to do, but hey, nothing was going to stop me.

We went thru the pain and sadness of telling our families — both Hillary's and my parents live within fifty miles of here. I expected my mom to take the news well. She was disconsolate. I expected Hillary's mom to fall apart. She was absolutely fine.

So much for expectations.

I wrote a long letter, somewhat similar to the one I sent to all of you, to let my practice folks know our plans. Writing the letter was fine, and I was happy with it. The evening before I was to distribute the letter, I reread it. Everything suddenly sank in to a level I had not previously allowed things to reach. I bawled like a baby for hours. Fifteen years of practice passed before my eyes. The babies, the hugs, the healings, the love; I laughingly reflected on how attached I still was. Yes, they can get on without me. Yes, it's chiropractic they need and not me. Yes, I am free to choose where and how to serve. Yet I could not, for the life of me, figure out how I was going to face Alex Barksdale.

Alexandra Signey Barksdale is the cutest, sweetest, most sensitive little girl in my practice. She's been calling me Dr. Stewy for five years, since she was four years old. How do you tell someone like that you are leaving? Well, the Universe spared me for a few days.

Strong in my intention to leave, we went ahead and started distributing the letter. The first gentleman got pissed off. It got worse from there. I spent the afternoon in tears. I hadn't adjusted anyone while crying since I was in Panama! I couldn't believe it. There were people who had only been with us a month or so who were hysterical! It was like attending my own funeral! I should add, there was lots of encouragement, too. Yet a huge seed of doubt entered my mind and hung there like a tremendous storm cloud, ready to burst forth with thunder and lightning and buckets of rain. Still, I hung tough, and gave out the letter for another couple of tear filled days.

Thank God, Alex was down in San Francisco visiting her grandmother. Her dad came in and I told him that for some reason, Alex was the one I was dreading the most.

He asked, "Why, do you think she can't handle it?"

"It's not her I'm worried about," I replied. "It's me!!"

The weekend came and the cloud erupted. Things became incredibly clear. I had been seeing only two possible paths: my practice or my dream.

In attending my own funeral, I rediscovered that my

I rediscovered that my practice was a huge part of my dream.

I guess I needed to be willing to let go of everything, to find out that I didn't want or need to.

practice was a huge part of my dream. I remembered how special it is. How special my practice folks are. How much we have accomplished, and how much we have impacted our community. More importantly, how much we haven't yet accomplished. I thot of the couple from New Zealand who spoke in England, who adjusted a third of the 1500 babies born in their town the previous year. I thot of all the babies still being inoculated right here in my town. I thot of the alarming state of principled chiropractic right here in its nation of birth. I thot of everything I was putting my wife and daughter thru. I thot of all kinds of things I had chosen to ignore. I had equated my dream and the things I wanted to do with England, and I realized that I could do them all here.

Incredibly, in less than a week, I went from "nothing will stop me from going" to "nothing will get me to go." My mind started in on me, calling me a weenie and some other choice things. I told it to shut up, because I had already done all the hard and scary stuff! And besides, I realized my ego was *mostly what had driven me to go in the first place. I thot it was my heart, and I've learned I still need some work in discerning which voice is which. God has planted me here, and here is where I'll stay for now. There is much work to be done. This process has greatly clarified the areas of work that are most necessary.*

By the time Alex came in the following week, I had already begun telling everyone I wasn't going to England. This was a lot more fun. As one fifteen-year member of my practice said, "The next time you want to know how much we appreciate you, why don't you just ask?" I told her I didn't think that would've worked as well. I guess I needed to be willing to let go of everything, to find out that I didn't want or need to.

I may take a little time off, and then return to this wonderful practice and community to continue the things we've begun. And at the same time, I will embark on the rest of my dream: helping to promote and save the chiropractic principle, and helping chiropractors to share that principle, thru speaking, writing, and perhaps coaching.

To all of you who have sent your encouragement and support, by email or thru the ethers, I am deeply touched and appreciative. Please do not stop sending your prayers. To all of you that frankly don't give a damn about this or my previous letter, I can understand that, too. Somewhere along the way I chose to openly share my feelings with anyone who cares to read or listen, and I continue to learn volumes about myself in the process.

In the meantime, I am ecstatic to be a chiropractor,

*Now I realize I have become a bridge…
between different worlds, between earth and heaven, between the Twinkies and the Spirit…
where earth meets heaven there is magical creation and manifestation, and I believe we are all here to create our dreams and to manifest love and beauty.*

wherever I happen to be. Take good care of this magnificent thing we have, and take good care of the Alex's in your own practices. I realize that Alex was a symbol of everything I love about my practice, and I hope to hear her children call me Dr. Stewy some day.

♥   ♥   ♥

Chapter 3:

Heaven or Earth?

"Beyond the Alps lie more Alps,
and the Lord alps those that alps themselves."
Groucho Marx

I've always been fascinated by bridges... and more than a bit afraid of them ever since seeing that video of the Bay Bridge collapsing during the 1989 earthquake. To this day I haven't the faintest notion of how they build one, and I would be embarrassed to share the ways my imagination pictures it done—how do they hold their breaths that long?

Growing up in New York City, bridges were a part of life. Only the Bronx is on the "mainland," so to get just about anywhere from Queens meant crossing a bridge. And while the differences between the banks spanned by some bridges didn't seem to warrant the effort involved in building them, crossing most bridges *brot* a dramatic change in feeling and energy.

Such warm memories. Leaving on vacation in the summer to upstate New York or to New England

Chiropractic provided a bridge and I rediscovered my heart.

Each chiropractic adjustment blurs the imaginary distinction between flesh and spirit, and clears the way for people to step into their own bridge-ness.

Each adjustment allows a connection to something greater, bigger and wiser.

always felt like a daring escape as we crossed the Triborough Bridge. I would be immersed in daydreams about fresh air, trees, mountains, and other things that New Yorkers are deprived of; feeling the gaze of the skyline on my back. A few miles later—which sometimes took an hour or so as we weren't the only ones escaping the city—we would pass Yankee Stadium, the last outpost. Ah, freedom. The energy would be a tad different, however, on the return trip, and my dad in particular, undoubtedly saddened by the prospect of going back to work, would go into Mr. Hyde mode as we crept back over the same bridge.

But my favorite bridge, by far, was the 59th Street Bridge, the link to Manhattan. Crossing this bridge *brot* an indescribable thrill as "the city" beckoned. The huge buildings loomed larger and closer as the traffic crawled along, reminding me that on the other side the pace was quicker and the stakes were larger; nothing was the same. Less than a mile in length, in many ways this bridge connected two different worlds. (Bear with me as

I reminisce, I'm going somewhere with this.)

In my spiritual journey, I am often confused as to which world I live in, the material or the spiritual. *Now I realize I have become a bridge.* In what I am and in what I do.

I am a bridge *between different worlds, between earth and heaven, between the Twinkies and the Spirit,* between the pygmy and the Giant, between the head and the heart. It is apparent to me that *where earth meets heaven there is magical creation and manifestation, and I believe we are all here to create our dreams and to manifest love and beauty.*

I spent many years digging out a huge gulf between head and heart. Then I stood on the head side gazing in many different and useless directions as the other side of the gap seemed to disappear in fog. When *chiropractic provided a bridge and I rediscovered my heart,* for a while I forsook the head side, declared war on it, and reveled in my spiritual self-importance. Regardless of which direction I chose to travel between the worlds, it seemed there was always a stiff toll to pay. So now I've decided on a truce, and I'm working on accepting and loving all my sides. Love is indeed the carpool lane on the bridge that I am. For now, I am content being a bridge.

At the same time, what I do provides a bridge for others to use:

Each chiropractic adjustment blurs the imaginary distinction between flesh and spirit, and clears the way for people to step into their own bridge-ness.

Each adjustment allows a connection to something greater, bigger and wiser.

*Each adjust-
ment delivered
with love, helps
bridge the gap
of emptiness
and separation
that many
people
perceive.*

*I am not
responsible
for what the
traveler will
find on the
other side,
only for
facilitating
their passage.*

*Each adjustment delivered with
love, helps bridge the gap of emptiness and separation that many
people perceive.*

I serve by offering a bridge,
spanning across one's fears and
doubts, to a whole different world
of wholeness and holiness. To
Innate. Layers of interference and
sundry masks are shed every time
this bridge is crossed, and a different
level of vibration and energy is
attained. I offer a bridge for others
to find their own power, their own
self-awareness, and their own
purpose. *I am not responsible for
what the traveler will find on the
other side, only for facilitating
their passage.*

To be maximally effective as a
bridge, I must remember that a
bridge does not attach to the person
that crosses over, does not fear
rejection from anyone, does not
fret over someone's personality or
finances or health condition, does
not alter its purpose depending on
appearances, and certainly never
attempts to figure out the benefits
that might come with the crossing.

A bridge serves the purpose for
which it was created, and that's

more than enough. (I kind of like the "ugh" in that word, for some reason.)

Just as bridges need to be maintained—they sort of forgot about that with the 59th St. Bridge—I need to nurture the bridge that I am with love. If I send love and only love across my bridge, then what returns is the fulfillment of my dreams and the answer to my prayers. If I open my heart fully and use my head (instead of it using me), and pour out my deepest and highest Self onto that bridge, the universe opens to me. If I continue to become more of a bridge myself, people can continue to cross me on their paths for a long, long time. Some will and some won't, and that's OK. I rest easily knowing I'm just the bridge and even one crossing changes lives.

Stop, in the name of love, before I lose my mind. What a great loss that would be. How does one go about finding a lost mind? Hire a private investigator? Put an ad in the paper and plaster flyers all over town?

Lost: one solid tho sometimes over imaginative and controlling mind. Handle with care. Reward offered if you could fix it up a little first. Otherwise you'll be very happy to return it to me and perhaps even give me a reward for taking it off your hands.

Of course I don't remember who I am or where you can find me or why I even want it back to begin with. If you don't believe me, read the rest of this book. You will then be convinced of the validity of this information.

My whole path is about losing my mind and finding my heart. I lose it daily in Hillary and Ari's love. I lose it in the moonbeams and the sun clouds. I lose it in the wide-open spaces, in the spider webs, in the dark woods, and in the woodchuck chuck. She sells seashells by the seashore, and I sell my soul when my mind is in control. So I'll set it adrift in one of her seashells and see where it ends up. It may encounter the ghost of Jimmy Hoffa floating on the ethers in Poughkeepsie. Then again it may fly up, up, and away in a beautiful balloon. Or maybe the world is my oyster and my mind is the pearl. Pearl Bailey might know, but I think she may be playing Hello Dolly in the big theatre in the sky.

Losing my mind is the order of the day. Order now and pay no shipping as the *Schmootz Brigade* ships out. Are you listening, oh momentous turds-of-petty-osity? Are you shivering in your hip waders, knowing your time is short? Well, not to worry, you'll always have a job—a cushy position in the firm.

My whole path is about losing my mind and finding my heart.

Innate is not your enemy... It loves you.

Because I believe in hiring the handicapped, you'll always be part of the team and I do not plan on throwing you out in the street. But here are the rules: you can offer suggestions without attachment and without hitting me below the self-esteem belt. And veto power is mine, so you can't turn me into one of your sh-t briquettes for turning down your suggestions.

Speaking of suggestions, I have one for you. Why don't you try sitting back and enjoying my journey to Spirit? Maybe you'd enjoy the energy and clarity. Maybe you'll spin around in your illusory vortex and help me maim our past programming with the fists of Truth and Light. Join with me on this crusade of becoming Innate's vessel. *Innate is not your enemy, my friend. It loves you.* It created you to police our day-to-day survival stuff in this world. It wants to show you the futility of attempting separateness. It wants you to be a rock of being for me in times of stress and survival; but it also wants you to be interested in our highest good, which includes unity, connection, right relationship, and service without attachment. You know—all that stuff you failed in school? And when I invariably make mistakes along the way, let that remind you that I am no longer the good little boy, and it's good for me to leave a few "wrong jobbies" around. That way you get to see some of your offspring abandoned by Innate so you can realize the futility of your unencumbered reproduction. Do you get the idea or do I have to clout you with a beanbag chair and love beads?

For some reason this all reminds me of the Oktoberfest in Bavaria. Those ladies may be able to lift 136 beer steins in each hand, but they can't lift even one Howard Stein with their tongues, now can they? And even if they could, can you imagine the hilarity of such a sight?

If you read further you will discover that there is very little to discover, but a lot to uncover, and an incredible amount to forget. So forget everything I said and uncover the blanket, because beneath it is a significantly scant population of bed mites and pillow maybes. They were there a minute ago but had to leave with their huge entourage because the night air was getting chilly. They rounded up the usual suspects, but just as they suspected, there weren't any. So they rounded up the corners instead and now we actually have boxing rings that are really rings. See what I mean about this mind?

Not convinced? Well... I think that the way to a man's heart is *thru* his rib cage and sternum, and if you think you'll get there by going *thru* the stomach, you must be a terrible Samurai warrior with very little background in anatomy. If the corn is really green, how

If you read further you will discover that there is very little to discover, but a lot to uncover, and an incredible amount to forget.

Ridiculous you say? It's about time.

Everyone of us is looking to love and to be loved and to find meaning in this big mess.

We can help each other bridge the gap between heaven and earth.

could you pick the Jolly Green Giant out from the really tall ears? Are they listening? You be the judge. So be ready to accept bribes and return favors and look honest. Are we supposed to not tell lies on Lincoln's Birthday? If so, why do we celebrate it on a day that wasn't even his birthday? Honest Abe wouldn't have liked it, but he was too busy anyway writing short speeches that would become immortal. *Ridiculous you say? It's about time.*

If you were seeking great literature, what are you doing here? Maybe the food is good, or maybe you just like my legs.

I really know so very little. Just a glimmer of truth at times. But the glimmer grows into sparks of light and love. The sparks ignite darkened fringes of doubt and past programming, and those burn and in turn fire the furnace of my quest for more truth. And on and on it goes to infinity, wherever that is.

We're all such lonely slugs in the cesspool of existence, *everyone of us looking to love and to be loved and to find meaning in this big mess*. It's such a beautiful mess and such a loving cesspool.

We help clean it up every time we remember who we are and who everyone else is. *We can help each other bridge the gap between heaven and earth.*

So I connect with that connection and I stay connected like super glue to ignore the Post-it Notes of the illusory past. Who cares what has gone on before except maybe Kodak and Memorex?

♥   ♥   ♥

CREAM PIE

*I feel like a cream pie poised
against society's face,
A thorn in the side
of the status quo,
Semi-awake amongst the
sleepwalking throngs
Going merrily along in
their suffering.*

*Yes, the world must remain
free to drift and dream,
But I can gently
elbow it in the ribs,
And nudge it off its
comfortable perch,
To be lovingly reset
by the Great Mystery.*

*But first it behooves me
to look within,
To take stock and fill
the cracks with love.
My wholeness sets the
Universe to quiver,
From sub-quark to distant galaxy.*

*The truth then erupts
from depth of being,
Unmindful of its
ultimate destination.*

The journey is the path of freedom
To hearts that are unchained and ready.

Let us allow nothing to
tarnish Innate's thots,
Tho they flee like burglars in the night.
Let us pursue them above all else
and find our Selves,
For therein lies the Divine.

Let us walk in the glow
of our missions of service,
Playing hide and seek with the world.
Let us dance in the flow of Creation,
And belt out our innermost tunes.

Many times in the past, when describing my chiropractic experiences in Panama, I've mentioned that during those missions I'd checked my brain in at immigration and didn't pick it up again until I left the country. Therefore, for a week at a time, I was able to remain in a blissful, brainless state, allowing my body to be used by God, and my gifts to be fully expressed. I was able to love unconditionally, to give myself away, to share my full power in service. I was able to bear witness to the majesty of the chiropractic adjustment delivered with no agendas or expectations or desires for recompense, and to see the miracles that inevitably resulted. And when I've managed to keep my brain from driving its doubting, whining stake thru the heart

*No longer
do I expect
my meditation
practice, or
the other
things I do in
preparation, to
suddenly and
miraculously
silence the
pitiful tennis
match of thots
that bounce
between past
and future,
between good
and bad,
between heaven
and a hard
place in my
head.*

*There's nothing
to figure out.
It's about
unlearning…
It's about
surrendering.*

of my mission here in my own practice, I've experienced the same things.

Coincidence? Heck no. It's the Law.

As long as I can remember, my mentor has implored me to stop thinking. I think I finally know what he means. It's not that we can really stop thinking. Even thinking about not thinking is still thinking. Since my brain apparently intends to remain firmly ensconced inside my skull, and also apparently intends to continue in its incessant chatter, I've decided to accept that.

No longer do I expect my meditation practice, or the other things I do in preparation, to suddenly and miraculously silence the pitiful tennis match of thots that bounce between past and future, between good and bad, between heaven and a hard place in my head. There are, of course, times when the match is like Centre Court at Wimbledon, and other times when it's like a quiet game of backyard badminton. But the match goes on. And the value of my spiritual work is that *now* I am often aware that I am not the match. I watch the match, I detach from the match; I even sometimes enjoy the match. Quite comical it is, really. Regardless of the score, I know that the match is not what or who I am.

In this state, instead of "thinking" being a series of reactions and programmed, fear-based idiocies that bombard me from every angle and cling to me like burrs, "thinking" is an outpouring of my heart's song, and my brain assumes its true function as a receiving device for God's *thots*. I can control my dominant *thots*, and I can choose which ones to believe. I can see things as I wish them to be. I can focus on *thots* that further my mission. And I can dwell in love, connection and *one-ness,* free of doubts, lack, limitation, and judgment. Like in Panama.

There is no magic involved here and no magical way to get "there." There is really no "there" to get to. The spiritual dimension exists right here and right now, and nowhere else. It is reality. To connect with it I simply have to disconnect from the illusions I previously allowed myself to believe were reality. *There's nothing to figure out. It's about unlearning.* There's nothing to do. *It's about surrendering.* There's nothing to buy, beg, borrow or steal.

It's about love: loving myself enough to know that I am Spirit, that I am whole, that I am powerful, and that I am fully capable of creating my dreams *thru* my intentions, because I am a child of God. I live in heaven and on earth simultaneously. I am not what I think I am, and I am not my *thots*. My *thots* can either serve me or destroy me; it's my choice. *I can't stop thinking, but I can create a masterpiece of loving thots that create beauty and serve everyone, including me.*

Descartes was wrong. "I think, therefore I am" is so much bullsh-t. "I am, therefore I think" is closer to the truth. Still closer is, "I am, even *tho* I think." I am, and that's a beautiful thing to think about.

♥   ♥   ♥

I can't stop thinking, but I can create a masterpiece of loving thots that create beauty and serve everyone, including me.

Chapter 4:

You Only Hurt The Ones You Love?

Zeppo: *Dad, I'm proud to be your son.*
Groucho: *My boy, you took the words right out
of my mouth. I'm ashamed to be your father.*

A long time ago I heard Wayne Dyer share that his
wife once asked him, "Wayne, how come you show
the world your holiness and you only show me your
ass-holiness?"

I have often pondered the reasons behind that,
because I do exactly the same thing. Not my dog,
Blue. He reserves any hostility for strangers. I take
mine out on those I love the most. Listening to some
things I say to my family, it would be difficult to
believe they were coming from the same mouth that
otherwise tends to utter such pearls of wisdom and
love. Such is the gift of having a brain larger than a
golf ball.

This issue of wanting to be nicer with my family
has nibbled at the cheese of my awareness longer than
any other, and it has been a constant source of left

hooks with which my mind beats me up.

It's amazing how sometimes we can be in absolute union and communion as a family, joined as one in an eternal dance *thru* this life and *thru* the cosmos, and other times we can all sound very much as if we hate each other. Deep down I know this family rocks with love and respect that transcends the petty lunacies that invariably show up from our respective *Schmootz Brigades*, which truly enjoy flinging the choicest dung in each others' faces just to be sure we remember how frail and human we are. But I'm getting pretty tired of the flinging.

And on we go, trying to see the truth. Much of the time I don't see it. I look out *thru* these portals of light and think I am seeing but it is merely the canvas of my imagination. I need to look inward to truly see.

So we work together as a family, joining forces with our Innates to drive onward to our utmost destinies with all our flags unfurled and our artillery booming and our entire armamentaria on display for

My life is too divine for Andy Devine to ridicule, and certainly too wonderful and full of joy for me to live it in a trance.

Even in the darkest times, the work reminds me that I am alive and vibrant and feeling and in my body if not altogether in my right mind.

the world to see, follow, love, hate or whatever it's going to do. I suppose that's all we can do. Sometimes I remember—more and more, I'd like to think. I'd like to think—that's the problem.

When I'm thinking, I'm about as effective at remembering as a blindfolded rhesus monkey is at performing minor surgery. Sure, he'd probably be as good as most surgeons, but what does that have to do with my issue with family? I'm glad you asked! Not that you really give a damn, but here goes: *My life is too divine for Andy Devine to ridicule, and certainly too wonderful and full of joy for me to live it in a trance.*

Indeed, yesterday when things were getting unconscious between Hillary and me, I walked away. Not so much in anger as from a conscious decision to leave it for another time when we are both more awake and more aware of our true relationship and feelings for each other. Hil, I hope you realized that, and you're not holding on to stuff, and I'm sorry I didn't just hug you and laugh at/with you.

Almost thirty years we've been together and you'd think by now that whenever we started getting caught up in the futility of words and of being right, we'd simply lie down and make love. Twenty-seven years and it seems like the blink of an eye, and yet I can't imagine anything before. There was no before, only togetherness *thru* eternity, so let's get as much learned together this time around to make this time around as wonderful and magical and beautiful as it can be—and also to make the next time around a little easier!

Ah, what joyous work it has been, *tho. Even in the*

We belong together...to discover the things that we still haven't learned to unconditionally love about ourselves.

Things like happiness, love, joy...are built into the system.

darkest times, the work reminds me that I am alive and vibrant and feeling and in my body if not altogether in my right mind.

Let's go together. Let's walk, hands held, heads uplifted and toward each other and toward the Divine. You and I, my beloved that is my Beloved. *We belong together* —if only to change the world and ourselves—*to discover the things that we still haven't learned to unconditionally love about ourselves,* so we can open our hearts and become zero. Together. The race is on and it looks like we'll enjoy the race whether we win or place, as long we continue to show up.

Sipping my coffee here in paradise, I am reminded of the futility of driving in the rain without windshield wipers. So if you think you can do it, you must either be from Seattle or you have delusions of grandeur that will someday be lost in a sea of foam and spray.

Anyway, Christmas is finally over and we did the annual January celebration of it in Carson City, Nevada. My folks are so happy it defies all pessimistic views of relationships. Of which there are many, especially tucked away inside my little brain. But what of my own relationship?

Is happiness a byproduct of services rendered? *Au contraire!* Sorry, I'm practicing for a trip to Quebec... happiness is not a byproduct of anything. Byproducts, not referring, of course, to those found in dog food — the character of which has long been a mystery to me — come from the brain. They usually only manifest themselves in things that are quite the opposite of *things like happiness, love, joy,* etc., which *are built into the system.* Those are already in the hard drive or the motherboard or the brotherhood or whatever, and you have to buy the other software if you want anything else. So don't bother, because it will only bring suffering following the installation. And besides, the software will become obsolete in a matter of moments, and you will continually have to upgrade. What a world.

On another note, this one being a C sharp, I believe, all is well. Can you believe it? Not that there is nothing my brain can conjure up to annoy itself — it can certainly do a great imitation of a dog chasing its own tail. I've always wondered, what would the dog do if it ever caught its tail? And what, pray tell, would we do if we ever caught up with our own brain? Would we make it walk the proverbial plank? How about elective lobotomies? Could they ever become as popular as boob or nose jobs? Tummy tucks? How about a tummy tuck with your lobotomy today so at least you can look really good while you drool and sell pencils on the street corner? You don't care, you say? Well good, you're getting the idea.

Good morning, *Schmootz Brigade*. I hope you're sitting down, because I have news for you. Your services are no longer required. We've replaced you with a new crop of recruits who don't yet know about my weaknesses and limitations. Get the picture? Move on and crystallize your efforts into something useful—like climbing Mt. Everest wearing roller skates. Go forth and divide and subtract yourselves from this scene, because I have seen how wonderful things can be without you. The entire *Schmootz Brigade* fell into the Sea of Love today and the brigadiers were last seen drying themselves with big sheets of toilet paper. Apparently they aren't dead, and I'm sure I'll be banishing them again. OK, I guess you can stick around, but forget about getting top billing.

And good morning to you, too, Hillary, you sure look lovely upon first arising. Like a sleepy toddler, except you walk better. I do love you, and as I was trying to say

I made the intention at our last personal development workshop to be as nice as my dog.

earlier, our family relationship provides multiple opportunities for me to remember my innate happiness. Perhaps more importantly, it provides multitudinous opportunities to help me discover the viruses in my hardware that make me forget.

This all has come to a head, so to speak, since getting the news yesterday that Ari is officially "going out" with someone of the male persuasion. Yes, it has finally happened. And *tho* no one, Ari included, seems to know exactly what that means, it feels rather large nonetheless. Indeed, the best I can say about the whole thing is that we are open in our communication about the matter, and I was able to relate some ridiculous "wisdom" to her about the nature of relationships. "Yes, darling, this is the best of times and the worst of times," I droned, as she looked at me with patience and that look of, "Uh huh, Dad, here we go again."

She is so beautiful, and romantic adventures with her as the co-star are as difficult to visualize as ones involving my parents. No, come to think of it, they are not quite so hard to visualize, much to my chagrin. *Oy!*

Poor Blue has been a nervous wreck. Ever since *I made the intention at our last personal development workshop to be as nice as my dog*, I find myself staring at him a lot, observing his reactions and basically trying to figure out what makes him tick. He doesn't dig it at all. He'll stare back at me, apparently trying to determine what he did wrong. When I don't say or do

He lives to please. Nothing makes him truly angry. He never judges today's walk against yesterday's. He bears no grudges, no resentments, no complaints, no addictions, no conceit, and no self-pity. He appears to have no ego to speak of...

How can I ever be like that?

anything, he keeps coming over to me, expecting to be petted or expecting us to go out for a walk or expecting whatever it is he expects. And since I've intended to be as nice as he is, I've been doing a lot of petting and walking. I've had to become sneakier in my observations, and *thru* them I've determined that he really is nice. *He lives to please. Nothing makes him truly angry. He never judges today's walk against yesterday's. He bears no grudges, no resentments, no complaints, no addictions, no conceit, and no self-pity. He appears to have no ego to speak of,* and basically he has been pissing me off. *How can I ever be like that?* Granted, I can certainly be nicer, especially with my family, and indeed I have even found myself asking the perhaps blasphemous question, "What would Blue do?" But can I really be like him? Do I need to eat hard, dry and disgusting dog food and nothing else? Do I need to accept, integrate, deny or obliterate my rather large ego?

Do I really need a lobotomy?

Last Friday rolled around bringing with it nearly twelve hours in the office (including another of my twice a week, marathon health talks), *and* I was faced with the prospect of: leaving my house at 9:30 p.m.; a 90 minute drive to Reno for a 12:30 a.m. flight to Dallas; with a two and one-half hour layover there; then a flight to Toronto arriving at noon local time. All for me to speak for a couple of hours at 8 PM the next day. I can't even begin to describe how little I wanted to go. I even went so far as to invent some excuses to get out of it, thinking the whole time, *Blue would never have allowed himself to get into this situation*—which didn't help. I went ballistic on my ego, blaming it for getting me to want to speak in Toronto. But voices in my head kept murmuring about abiding by commitments, and people needing to hear my message, which is part of my mission. Not to mention the fact that my ego still slobbered over the idea of speaking where some of my teachers and mentors had spoken before. So off I went.

The talk went well, even *tho* I had only about two hours sleep in two nights. My ego was doing a gracefully refined tap dance across the dance floor of my consciousness as people came up and thanked me. (Astair-esque. "A-stair" as in without steps? Hmm.)

Then an amazing thing happened. A young man named Colin emerged from the shadows, tears in his eyes, identified himself as a University of Toronto philosophy student. He proceeded to ask me about the meaning of life. I could tell he was lost, so I shared some principles of chiropractic philosophy and gifted him with my first book. I gathered my belongings, said some final good-byes, and left to return to my hotel.

Did Innate create my ego and does It use it to get me to do stuff that is essential for the plan?

Can I see myself as already whole, healed and perfect? Can I really see that in others until I see it in myself?

Are we really all angels for each other in this magnificently designed life?

There was a thunderstorm raging after six weeks of no rain, so I had to detour on my route back to the hotel. I passed a tall column, and leaning on the far side of the column, reading my book, was Colin. We talked for an hour—he was indeed lost. He had been experiencing what he considered some form of divine guidance, but was unable to accept it. He questioned it; he tried to figure it all out; and he plunged into a deep depression. I remember thinking, *he could greatly benefit from hanging out with Blue.* Then I said something to him, which I can't even remember, and he burst into tears.

"I'm feeling very moved by what you're saying," he admitted. At that precise moment, a lightning blast went off directly over our heads, and a nearly simultaneous thunderclap scared the sh-t out of both of us. We looked at each other *thru* teary eyes and laughed about the exclamation point that God just placed after his sentence. It was right out of the film *The Natural*. Then he shared with me how he attended church earlier in the evening, for the first time in his life; and while there, he was loudly and clearly directed to get up and go to the auditorium where I was speaking and where he would meet an angel. Wow. We hugged as he told me he had always hoped his angel would turn out to be a beautiful girl, and I returned to my hotel room to subsequently keep my sleepless streak alive.

As always, I am left with multitudinous questions. *Did Innate create my ego and does It use it to get me to do stuff that is essential for the plan?* Like getting me to Toronto? Do I really have faults and weaknesses? Do I really have free will? Do I really want to be like Blue, or am I already an angel just the way I am? *Can I see myself as already whole, healed and perfect? Can I really see that in others until I see it in myself?* Is there such a thing as separation of any kind, or does my brain just continually cut slices out of wholeness? Is the whole thing rigged? *Are we really all angels for each other in this magnificently designed life?*

Do I really have to have any of these questions answered? Or do I simply get to wonder and experience as I venture on my path, enjoying every step?

It's Groundhog Day. I think I saw my shadow this morning, and I'm not sure if that means the winter of my awareness is destined to hang around for six more weeks, or if what I saw was actually only a mirage? My shadow side is becoming more and more of a source of great humor—or at least Good Humor, and the ice cream man cometh.

Yesterday, Hillary reminded me of one of the more comical things I do. We were washing dishes together (a trick in itself), when she suddenly and inexplicably stepped directly, and with full weight, onto my broken little toe. In the process of getting off, hastened by my blood-curdling scream, she sort of spun around and ground it even more into the floor with her heel. The funny part was that after I emerged from my coma, I found that *she* was angry with *me!* Imagine that, as if it were my fault or something. Sorry, dear, I really shouldn't have placed my toe right under your foot like that. My apologies. I hope I didn't hurt the undersurface of your foot too much. But then I realized *I do the same exact thing*.

I remember being angry with Hillary on many occasions related to her ailments or inability to sleep. Indeed, *nearly every time I get angry with my family lately I get the realization "sooner or later" that I do the exact same thing that I'm getting angry with them about.* I'm happy to say it seems to be getting sooner and sooner. *About*

Nearly every time I get angry with my family lately I get the realization "sooner or later" that I do the exact same thing that I'm getting angry with them about.

about... If I haven't asked this before, why is it so hard not to end a sentence with a preposition? Do you think it's because of our education system? Or do we blame them for too much already? Why can't the English learn to speak?

When I find myself getting angry at Hillary about her various afflictions, as if they were some sign on her part of weakness or something or other, is it because of the *effects* that affliction may have upon me? Seems likely. How nuts! It may or may not *affect* me, but I view her as responsible as if it was something she controlled or premeditated. And I make it all about me. That's a lot of presumption on my part.

And just yesterday, too, I nearly lost my cool upon seeing Ari eating a muffin or something at her desk in the office, spraying crumbs all over the floor like a crop duster. Hillary actually had to remind me of all the meals I've devoured standing at the counter or roaming around the house, and all the times she's had to get angry at me for *eating without a plate or napkin*. My, my—that was Gulliver's favorite expression in the movie, by the way. I'm sure that makes your day.

The *Schmootz Brigade* apparently likes to be democratic in whom it beats up, alternating between pumping me up into the illusion of power by having me get angry with family, and then turning around and eviscerating me for doing the same things I had gotten angry about with them. And of course for getting angry with them. Is it any wonder the world is so insane? Maybe Mel Brooks is right, things would get better if the earth finally stopped spinning so much and everyone wasn't so dizzy!

What happens to all these memories that stir or lie dormant in my soul?

Things change; kids grow; people age and die. It simply points once again the eternity of each moment, and to the sanguine luxury of rhetorical nonsense known as the past and future — fun to dally in at times, but not real.

I'd like to develop this idea further, someday, especially the getting angry at the weirdest of things and times, because there's a wealth of insanity as well as clues to the solution in there somewhere.

Sometime... Somewhere, over the rainbow, skies are blue, and perhaps there's also a pot of gold waiting for the Robert E. Lee. In the interim, the monkey wrapped his tail around the flagpole and saluted with the wrong appendage, thusly violating our Constitution, and they'll have to see about having it cleaned up. Then it'll be a lot less fun, but at least it won't be banned. Yes, and then all you young sports fans can clamor and moan about the lack of Internet software contained within flak jackets across the nation's capital or is it Capitol. I forget. I forget myself often, which indeed becomes the highlight of that particular day, because my self is utterly forget-table. My Self, Innate, on the other hand, is, in the words of Nat King Cole, kind of like Jack Frost nipping at your nose.

Ha — fooled you there, didn't I?

♥   ♥   ♥

My Grandma Debbie passed on early yesterday morning at age 96, and I feel relief, sadness, joy, frustration, and acceptance all at the same time. Yes, she's no longer suffering and all those other clichés. But the sadness comes from a time connection being severed. Her memories were tied in with her body and I'm not sure what happens to those. Her little stories and recollections of when I was little: who remembers them now? Since I have no clear memories of past lives, only glimpses and feelings and twitches of memorabilia, I have to assume the memories of this current life will be mostly lost as well. It surely would be nice to place them on deposit somewhere, or in someone, like Spock did with Bones McCoy in that Star Trek movie, only to be retrieved later on.

Really, *what happens to all these memories that stir or lie dormant in my soul?* Stuff like my third grade teacher's amazingly low hanging breasts. Does all of it go into the universal vault and become part of the race DNA? Can you imagine inheriting knowledge of Mrs. Schmidt's boobs? How earth shaking—literally! I guess memories join a long list of things that are not me. *Things change; kids grow; people age and die. It simply points once again* to *the eternity of each moment, and to the sanguine luxury of rhetorical nonsense known as the past and future—fun to dally in at times, but not real.*

Eternity is in each present moment. Debbie, I know we'll meet again in some dimension or form, and I am at least happy that I told you I loved you and thanked you for loving me while I sat with you and said goodbye. I'm so glad we had this closer connection for the past year, and more than anything that you got to know your great-grandchild and got to be touched by that pure bundle of joy.

Ari, I'm so impressed with your attitude and courage as you sat with Debbie to ease her passing. You are older than Debbie, aren't you? You will continue her genes and those memories and keep them alive, and I must say they're in good hands. Yes, it never ends.

And Hillary—you're unbelievably wonderful, too. You've been so great with Debbie all year and at the "end." Debbie really loved you and it was clear to see why. You helped her so much, and your energy in holding a vision of love for her made her a lot less fearful about her journey.

Anyway, goodbye Grandma. Thanks for the love and memories and those great longevity genes I hope I got.

This has also *brot* up the fact that we are all children. I'm thinking of my terrific parents, normally above average in the capability

The ones who know the least, but know they know the least, are the ones that most people think know the most.

department, who have been saddened and confused to the point of near ineptitude by this whole thing. Sometimes we're all as helpless as children, and so now they've turned to us, and it's OK. I'll turn to Ari and to others at times. We turn and turn and spin and evolve and we're all in this together. It's a wonderful deal because we're all just little kids trying to act grown up and responsible, and we really don't have a clue.

Some know this, which allows them to surrender and make choices based on their hearts. These are the people that lead and make an impact. *The ones who know the least, but know they know the least, are the ones that most people think know the most.* I want to be like them. Thanks for another lesson, Debbie. I'll see you in my dreams, and we can tell stories into the long night of eternity.

7:30 in the morning and I've been up for hours. Funny how things do change as one gets older. I used to sleep like a log, now I sleep like a baby—I'm up every 2 hours. And I used to sleep *thru* earthquakes. Now if someone sneezes within a half-mile radius of my bedroom, I'm up. Well, it's just one of those things. Just one of those crazy flings. And life is indeed crazy.

One element of craziness in the last few years has been the transition that both my wife and daughter have been undergoing; Ari has been becoming a woman, and Hillary has been slip sliding away into whatever comes after that. And I've got to tell you, Hillary's process has seemed a hell of a lot longer than

Like Einstein said, picture ten seconds sitting with your lover, and now picture ten seconds sitting on a hot stove, and you get the picture of relativity.

It's a completely different, brand new ball game every moment.

Ari's, *tho* I'm sure it really hasn't been. Part of that relativity thing right there. *Like Einstein said, picture ten seconds sitting with your lover, and now picture ten seconds sitting on a hot stove, and you get the picture of relativity.*

Both transformations have been somewhat traumatic for me.

The latest development in Ari's journey in this life has been the addition of an actual boyfriend, as mentioned previously. So this is what everyone was jokingly referring to all these years about having a daughter. But it's no joke! Talk about a torrent of *thots!* I'd be a little worried about her if she wasn't interested in boys, but now I get to worry about her a lot! Seeing them hugging each other is an indescribable thing: bittersweet, adorable, heart-rending, nostalgic, you name it. And knowing what I know about the nature of relationships, which isn't much, I've so far successfully avoided the tendency to give her a bunch of advice, and have been thrilled with her willingness to be open in her communication with us about it all.

Wasn't it just yesterday I held

her in one hand, and she looked at me with those penetrating blue-green eyes and stole my heart? Talk about relativity. She's become a beautiful young lady right under my nose, and even *tho* I've been watching it all, it has whizzed right by like a hurricane. I can almost feel my hair flying in the breeze, and wonder about my own changes during these past fifteen years.

What have I missed about myself? Again, it's one of those mysterious manifestations of Maya: my brain does its best to make it seem like nothing changes, and yet a brief assessment generally yields a completely different story. *It's a completely different, brand new ball game every moment.* I wonder if Ari feels any different than when she first began to walk or talk?

Now Hillary's deal, on the other hand, has been harder. I have often felt like saying what Archie Bunker told Edith during a similar process in their lives: "Edith, if you're going to change, go ahead and get it over with!" But alas, it doesn't work that way. So there have been extremely scary cycles of anxiety and sleeplessness and weird neurological symptoms for her, and *thru* the process there have been times when I've been a little petulant because my manhood wasn't stroked. I've been such a horny toad it's amazing I don't croak. Maybe Hillary's been staying away to avoid the warts? Anyway, with all this going on, we've managed to get into some incredibly ridiculous arguments about things that are not even worth remembering—must be why I don't remember them. I have tried to put myself in her shoes and besides my toes getting very cramped, it has been interesting.

So I've had to adjust to these phases because

Nothing is ever nearly as bad as the way I think about it.

When I serve God by giving away the gifts that God gave me—without strings attached—God takes care of me in perfect, abundant and unimaginable ways.

Do we really serve others or simply do things to serve our own ego?

otherwise the fireworks would be shooting across the skies of my life without a pail of water to dampen the heat. Just a few more things from which I've needed to attach-proof myself. I just coat myself with silicon and olive oil and slip and slide my way *thru* the Kling-ons of life. No Velcro on this guy. And it also feels like a pit of hell sometimes with all the choices I feel compelled to never make and to merely stress over—I know that it's just my brain activity, so shut up already! *Nothing is ever nearly as bad as the way I think about it.* Grow up? Or show up? Or throw up? Whatever. I know it's not me. I revel in the work of becoming more loving; especially with those I love the most. I watch the craziness of it all, occasionally going in for a dip that never refreshes, and sooner or later I will hopefully realize it's best to never jump in, but to engage in ceaseless prayer that will free me to love and serve and experience the *fantastic-osity* of every ditty of time. I love run-on sentences! They remind me of my life sometimes.

♥   ♥   ♥

Chapter 5:

Serving God or Serving Me?

Steward*: You might have some tomato juice,*
orange juice, grape juice, pineapple juice…
Groucho*: Hey, turn off the juice before I get*
electrocuted.

I've written and spoken *ad nauseum* about a subject I call "service without strings." Service for the sake of serving, as I've experienced in Panama and many times since, is the reason I offer chiropractic care in my office on a pay-as-you-can-afford basis, and have a donation box on the back of the front desk. I discovered in Panama that *when I serve God by giving away the gifts that God gave me—without strings attached—God takes care of me in perfect, abundant and unimaginable ways.*

But occasionally I still have doubts. I have been served so magnificently *thru* my service that I wonder if it's really possible to ever serve totally without strings.

Do we really serve others or simply do things to

serve our own ego? Do we serve our highest selves to be able to serve others with less ego-involvement? Or do we double fault and serve no one and no thing? I'd like to think that I'm at least becoming aware and present enough in each moment to overcome the old bear that keeps me down, keeps me small, keeps me doing and thinking things that I chose not to do or think any longer. Do and think, think and do. It's like a bridge game of lunacy played with four dummies. No wonder not much gets done. I get in my own way, and when I really move it's generally in your way.

Our ways are truly unique, but sometimes it seems really crowded near the center of this wheel of life. We know, as spokes on this wheel, that there's plenty of room near the periphery where we tend to live out our moments. So being out there, doing and thinking, *knowing that at the center we are one, connected in every way, helps me to do my thing in the most loving way.* And when I do the center is always available to me, and its gifts are always ready to shower upon me.

Knowing that at the center we are one, connected in every way, helps me to do my thing in the most loving way.

Find love in the giving, serving and loving.

The center is there and it's coming closer and it's here and it's happening—sorry, too late. Well, try again later, son, when your girlfriend dumps you and you aren't trying to impress anyone.

Who out there is not trying to impress someone? I suppose the best the old brain allows us is to try to impress ourselves. Yet, the possibility exists that we can grow into trying only to impress God. And maybe even to the point where we can serve without even trying to impress God? But serve simply because it's what we love to do! *Find love in the giving, serving and loving.* Loving love as a verb, and not caring about the verb's result. English grammar dictates that a verb is action—pure and simple. When we saw Dick and Jane run, for instance, did we care where they were going? Did we concern ourselves about whether anyone was necessarily impressed by all that running? Did their running change the world? Did it help anyone? Did it even help their own self-esteem? Well, if they loved to run, then yes on all counts. If they ran because someone told them to run, they should have walked instead.

Of course with the bases loaded, a walk IS a run.

I guess that settles it!

For much of my life, my ego had full command of my *thots*. Like a crazed sea captain, it terrorized the high seas of my consciousness, filling them with fear and self-loathing, making Awareness and Love walk the plank. I drifted with the tides of the external conditions

I was manifesting. I charged on without sextant or anchor *thru* calm and tempest. Life was unfair, meaningless, scary and only sometimes fun. My heading was ever turned in the direction of making someone like me. A jealous captain, I spent much time and energy judging others as to his or her potential to be threat or friend. I deemed many to be my betters, and placed them on pedestals, while simultaneously despising them for having things I apparently lacked. And despising myself for lacking them. Many others I labeled as "lesser," and I recruited them to be part of the crew so I could feel better about myself. In this way, I spent three and a half decades strapped to the mast like Ulysses hoping to escape the Siren's call—my ears were deaf to Innate's call.

When I awoke to the fact that my ego was not me, and only a bunch of electrochemical activity in my brain, it became the hated enemy. Some other "I"—or so I *thot*, began a search-and-destroy mission against Public Enemy #1. This other "I" blamed all the lack and self-sabotage and underachieving

I am not my ego, and I no longer hate it.

This truth affords me the gentleness and humor with which I now watch the unfolding of my existence.

that was my life on poor Ego. Limiting my power, keeping me small and afraid, impersonating a person, and many other items were on the indictment. This "I" mutinied and gained control of the rudder. Now I was on a different trip: my spiritual path.

I spent much time and energy judging others as to how far along that path they appeared to be. I now had different reasons to beat myself up—constantly acting differently than a "spiritual" person acts. You know, patient, accepting, loving, stuff like that. And, I frequently noticed the view from the bridge appeared to be pretty much the same as it was before. Hmmm... it finally occurred to me that this other "I" was possibly a new and improved I. But it was indeed one and the same. I dreamt of a different "I." The one I was beginning to know I really am—Innate.

The years pass faster than the sheep I used to count when I was younger. And my life is somehow catching up with my dream.

After all the work on self-awareness, all the searching and the questioning, all the growth and discovery and revelation that the chiropractic principle has *brot* to my life, this is where I am: I am full of sh-t and so is everyone else. I simply cannot escape the truth of it, and it brings me a deep sense of peace, and a blissfully satisfied smile. *I am not my ego, and I no longer hate it*. It most certainly is full of sh-t, but it is part of me, and part of this dance I do between heaven and earth. Part of being human. And it's OK. *This truth affords me the gentleness and humor with which I now watch the unfolding of my existence*. I am most assuredly entertaining. I now spend much time and energy having compassion for others, because I know they are full of sh-t, too; and I allow them the space to clean up their own, while I help remove interference to the manifestation of their highest selves. *I do the best I can at being true to my highest self.* I work toward spending more time and energy serving, loving, and being. I meditate with the intention of gaining more awareness of my *thots. I surrender to a deeper and deeper understanding and knowledge that I and the Father are One.* I use my ego to keep me motivated, and I use my sh-t to help me serve. I am full of sh-t and it's all perfect, because Innate is the captain, and the horizon looks almost unbearably beautiful from here.

I am flying back from speaking at the chiropractic college in Quebec—sitting in first class, by the way, and I'm full of doubts. I'm also full from the nice if not all-that-delicious dinner—in case I forgot to mention it, I'm sitting in first class! The doubts consist of

I do the best I can at being true to my highest self.

I surrender to a deeper and deeper understanding and knowledge that I and the Father are One.

Take a chance; it's only one life.

things that arise mainly because I'm always judging myself on performance and the like, and I always attempt to do so from others' perspectives. The good little boy is a role played to perfection most of my life. A first class act.

Back to Quebec.

I really love speaking and sharing my message, but I know that my ego is so deeply invested, it makes me doubt (what doesn't) if it's my real purpose. I've stated and written an intention to stick around the office more this year, and at times that feels good and right, but my ego doesn't exactly rest too much there, either. It rests while I'm adjusting, but in between and before and after and all those other times, it makes up for lost time—like a lover that's been too long denied. It then slobbers and salivates with attachments and approval seeking and all its other ridiculous but all-too-familiar games of chance. *Take a chance; it's only one life,* and who knows if it will last or if it will be first or if it will take the Bronze or take the Fifth? Or if you prefer, I can wash and dry your socks but it doesn't mean I love you or can even stand the sight of you. Yet, on the other hand one sock washes the other, and if you scratch my back I'll adjust yours...

Meanwhile, it was a good talk I gave in Quebec.

It was me and it was from my heart, and I know it had an impact. Is a book that impacts millions worth more than a talk that impacts one?

Speaking of books, the one I just read was really sad, The Forest House by Marion Zimmer Bradley. So much death and futility, and at the same time so much dignity and sacrifice and honor; and who knows which

*Hope
remains in the
loving and in
the residue it
leaves in
the sands
of time.*

*As I continue
to love
myself,
the doubts
vaporize.*

*My purpose
is to love
everyone, and
to serve them
all with my
gifts.*

is which and who is who? Destiny rears its ugly head and two more appear for every one you chop off. People will always be people who need people, even tho they end up hurting each other. In the book, as in life, you always root for the lovers, and other strangers step in to ruin it all. But *hope remains in the loving and in the residue it leaves in the sands of time.* And you thot that stuff in the sand was only fragments of granite eroded over eons? Well, amongst the granite bits are the souls of lovers forever entwined. The lovers in the book get their last laugh at the very end; and only their love for each other can make them laugh at that point, because all hell has broken loose. And we're supposed to feel good about it all, because now King Arthur can come along in a few hundred years and be involved in an even sadder story. Yikes! It's enough to make one turn to the horrors of the flesh—which sound particularly OK after that hot fudge sundae I just ate. First class ain't bad.

People are really, truly full of it. But I love them, even the ones I hate, because they're human. And, I suppose, that includes me. So, *as I continue to love myself, the doubts vaporize,* and Hall's Mentho-lyptus has advanced vapor action.

You know, if I just went on like this for 300 pages, they could use the book as some kind of test for psychosis or something. "Here, read this, and if you make it all the way *thru,* we'll really know you're nuts. Chock full of them, and no millionaire's money can buy you out of there. But at least you get to drink good coffee."

Hopefully you weren't looking for a book that was written in some sort of coherent fashion. Everyone does that, and the fashion of today is most certainly the rag of tomorrow. And the rag of today is even more certainly the reason I try to stay out of Hillary's way at her moon time. I hope nobody taped that remark! This book was taped before a live audience, and they all forgot to laugh when the "laugh" sign was held up, so we replaced them with you.

Have you noticed, while we're on the subject (if we were ever on one), that "the purpose of a man is to love a woman? And the purpose of a woman is to love a man? So come on baby let's talk today, come on baby let's play, the game of love." Man, they don't write 'em like that anymore, which is undoubtedly one of the finest pieces of news I've *thot* up in a long time.

Anyway, *my purpose is to love everyone, and to serve them all with my gifts.* whether or not it pleases the good little boy. There you have it, folks, the secret of life coming to you from right here on this plane—in first class, in case I forgot to mention it. If I keep on sitting in first class, how long do you think it would take me to get over the guilt I feel as all the coach passengers file by, stopping and starting in their long walk back to the cramped and underfed deal they're all about to experience for the next umpteen hours? Or, for that matter, to get over the almost irresistible tendency to want to trip them as they walk by?

When I was in college more than three decades ago (my God!), I was popular for three reasons.

First, I was a renowned herbalist, dealing exclusively with the smoke-able varieties, and was widely known for the quality of my wares.

Second, the seats around me during an exam were always a hot ticket, and to this day it amazes me how much imagination, creativity and energy went into the various methods of cheating that went on. Well, for some it beat studying, I guess. I remember during exams in the big lecture hall, when they passed out "A" and "B" tests so

The unfolding of my mission allows me to look at each excuse and confront it head on, and in the process I discover that it contains no power other than the power I put into it.

your partner on either side would have a different order to their questions, as soon as the proctor passed by there would be wholesale passing, sometimes throwing, of exams. Unbelievable! Kind of makes you wonder about those guys doing brain surgery, doesn't it?

Anyway and finally, *I was the master of excuses*. If you wanted to get out of something, I was your man. My excuses were juicy with pathos and could not be disputed. I knew because I had tried them all personally. Not only could you get out of the test or whatever, but you would have the teacher's sympathy as well. I even *thot* of publishing all of them as a book.

Yes, excuses have been, historically, the exhaust from the motor that drove me. Playing small... choked with fear... happy as long as everyone liked me... not making waves... the good little boy... the ideal citizen. Not much good to anyone, unless perhaps 1) you wanted to get stoned, 2) you didn't study for your test, or 3) you needed an excuse.

Now for the good news: I'm running out of excuses!

As I grow, most of the excuses for failing that I keep secreted away in the anals of my mind (no, that's not a misspelling), the ones that always seemed so valid, are tested and found wanting. *The unfolding of my mission allows me to look at each excuse and confront it head on, and in the process I discover that it contains no power other than the power I put into it.* I keep reminding myself that excuses are like leeches that suck the lifeblood out of my intention to serve. Actually, I take that back, and if there was a leech around I would apologize. At least a leech is real, and

*Excuses
live solely in
the outer world,
the world of
effect, and I no
longer choose
to hang out
there.*

*All I know is
that my life is
run more and
more by
something way
beyond my
puny intellect.*

has an important role to play (even if, for the life of me, I can't imagine what it is). An excuse is a phantom. A cowardly menace when your back is turned, it turns and runs like a frightened bunny when the light of awareness is cast upon it. An excuse is a self-fulfilling illusion, a futile exercise in self-pity and self-loathing. *Excuses live solely in the outer world, the world of effect, and I no longer choose to hang out there.* Innate doesn't need excuses. So when I find myself thinking up some excuse, I ask myself some simple questions:

"Can I make better use of this energy?"

"Wouldn't I rather focus on what's real?

"Am I not handcuffing Innate with this drivel?"

"Are you nuts?" That one tends to get my attention. Once my attention is on the miserable little excuse for an excuse, away it goes to hide in the shadows with the rest of the *Schmootz Brigade*. And away I go to serve my mission— maybe not quite as popular, but a lot more free to serve.

♥   ♥   ♥

I haven't touched a basketball in over four years. Believe it or not I was once a bit of a very minor legend, right out of the New York City school yards. For the past few months Innate has been nudging me back onto the court. So far, I've managed to avoid it, citing age and bad knees and oxygen tanks and some other truly unempowering excuses. Well, Innate most recently pulled out the two by four.

On consecutive days this week, I ran into three guys from my last basketball team, none of whom I had seen since our last game, over four years ago. Okay Innate, I'm heading out on the court.

Coincidence, you say? I chuckle at the *thot*. Law, I say. Simply the way It works. Manifestation, synchronicity, connection; call it what you will. *All I know is that my life is run more and more by something way beyond my puny intellect*. Something that flies in the face of logic and of everything I learned in school. Something that appears more and more as I open my heart. Something that dances with all of creation. Something we call Innate.

This past April was marked by the manifestation of several of my dreams. It was incredibly busy and incredibly balanced. It was also incredibly fulfilling and incredibly humbling. And it was all incredibly perfect—and that's the last "incredibly"—I promise.

The humbling part happened because I got a little cocky, I think. After a series of personal triumphs, I was aware my ego was beginning to prance around a bit. *Tho* I was keeping an eye on it, I know I forgot to

*I gave it
my best shot
and perhaps
one person got
the message.*

*"Take no
credit;
take no
blame."*

fully acknowledge the Source of my triumphs. I forgot whom it is I choose to serve.

Here's what happened.

For the past four years, I spoke at the local community college's Earth Day event. A rather small venue, but always fun. The large event in town for Earth Day is two days later at the Middle School, in which the entire community gets involved, and I'd always wanted to get on the stage for that one. This year, for some reason I wasn't invited to speak at the college. Could it be that last year I kind of got down on the educational system? Well, I put out a silent intention to speak at the Middle School. The morning of the big event one of my practice folks, who was involved in planning it, called and said, "Dr. Stew, we messed up and left an hour unplanned, could you possibly speak at 1 PM?" My ego went into full-scale self-celebration. Can you believe how I manifested that? Now the whole town gets to hear me! What a month!

Needless to say, it was a major fiasco. My mike kept cutting out—

we tried three different ones—and no one really wanted to listen anyway. They were more interested in low flow toilets, xerotrophic gardening (minimum use of pesticides), sustainable forest management and stuff like that. I attempted to shout my way into everyone's attention, pleading that we'd repeat Earth Day for another 333 years until we learned to heal ourselves, and I basically came off as a raving lunatic. I knew a bunch of people there, and several of them came to hug me after I gave up, but I know they simply felt sorry for me. Thanks, guys. Well, my ego began its old pattern of second-guessing itself and beating me up and wanting to dig a hole somewhere and have me crawl into it, and I finally woke up.

It was all perfect.

I gave it my best shot and perhaps one person got the message. AND I learned some invaluable lessons about humility and about how truly loving this Universe is.

One of my teachers used to quote DD Palmer, the founder of chiropractic, *"Take no credit; take no blame."* This applies not only to my adjusting, but also to my life. I like the part about not taking the blame a lot better than the credit part. I take responsibility, never blame.

And I allow myself to take a little credit: I take credit for asking for what I want instead of what I don't want; I take credit for the courage and awareness to make right choices and to sing my song; I take credit for the discipline to do the work, as a disciple to Innate. For allowing myself to be used as an instrument; for allowing myself to surrender to the perfection of life's flow; and for allowing myself to manifest my birthright of abundance, joy and love. The rest is not only out of my hands, it is out of my mind.

Out of my mind and in my heart is where I choose to be. Being in my heart brings the world and me closer to wholeness. Being in my heart brings me the experience of love—given and received. Being in my heart brings me a clearer view of the big picture. *Being in my heart brings me the balance between serving me and serving God.*

And being in my heart will bring me onto the basketball court really soon! Let's hope my heart holds up out there.

Out of my mind and in my heart is where I choose to be.

Being in my heart brings me the balance between serving me and serving God.

Chapter 6:

Chiropractic: Job or Adventure?

Groucho: *How would you like a job in the mint?*
Chico*: Mint? No, I no like-a mint. What other*
flavors you got?

Another paradox I have encountered, stewed over, and generally tiptoed around for many years is one I call "the belonging thing."

On the one hand, I crave a sense of belonging. Whenever I've seen a musical show, for instance, I've longed to be part of the chorus. And the paradox is that at other times, I have a deep longing to go it alone.

I don't know whether it's a case of not wanting to join a club that would have someone like me as a member, or whether deep down I realize that all groups develop a group mentality, viewing anyone outside the group as somehow wrong or inferior. Or maybe it's simply a case of remembering all the times people have let me down, and if you want something done, do it yourself and all that. I have generally gone solo on many a venture and adventure. I saw an ad for a venture once that said if I acted now, I would also receive a set of Ginsu knives, with a 50-year guarantee. When I called the toll free number, the company had already gone out of business. So much for groups.

Nowhere else but in chiropractic does this belonging issue become regurgitated more. I recently didn't attend the largest seminar gathering of chiropractors in the history of chiropractic—which spans almost 108 years now. And this thing about belonging has sort of come up again.

Often I feel alone in my beliefs, isolated like a tiny island in a sea of unconsciousness and medical thinking, and just as often I get off on the idea of my one-man crusade —two men, actually, if you include Hillary. I moan about the lack of like-minded chiropractors, especially in my geographic area. When I attend seminars I am always tremendously uplifted to realize I am indeed not alone, and there are warriors for the chiropractic principle everywhere, both among the seasoned veterans and the students.

All these paradoxes are just another example of the balance of things.

My brain flips the coin in the air and Innate catches it and promptly ignores the sides, because only It knows both sides are simply one.

Crazy. Well, you must be used to that by now. I certainly am.

You know, *all these paradoxes are just another example of the balance of things.*

Maybe my brain does the supreme balancing act? I can see it now, with 25 plates in one hand, whistling Waltzing Matilda and spinning the plates around on its nose. Wow, now it's standing on one toe, suspended in thin air, reciting the Gettysburg Address with one arm tied behind its back. Can you believe it? What an organ! Now it's playing the organ with both feet, while both cerebral hemispheres are playing bridge with two other dummies. Maybe I just have a sharp aptitude for seeing both sides of the coin, which my brain flips in the air and Innate catches... Man oh man, that's balance.

It seems that there is something to this balance thing, and after writing that last paragraph of nonsense, I'm still not sure what it is that does the balancing. So it must be Innate. My brain never seems to know what it wants, except perhaps the exact opposite of whatever it is that is going on. So... *my brain flips the coin in the air and Innate catches it and promptly ignores the sides, because only It knows both sides are simply one.* Which, by the way, is the loneliest number—but I hear it has a girlfriend now, which may change the situation...

Anyway, there are too many stops in this typing, and too many stops on this train, and I want to get off! It seems to be heading down a well-grooved track, and I forgot to check with my bookie before coming. On the right track or the wrong track, or on the wrong side of the tracks, my brain doesn't really care, as long as it

*The
universe
is putting on a
show written by
my thots,
starring a cast
of thousands
of fellow
travelers, and
directed by
God.*

*Thru
chiropractic I
caught a
glimpse of the
truth.*

*The answers
I was ready for,
only birthed
additional
questions.*

can continue to imagine it is running the show. And what a show it is! Complete with dancing girls and purple hippopotami. I am flabbergasted that I spelled that right. Hah!! (Yiddish Ha!) It is certainly not flowing today—kind of dammed up you might say. And frankly my dear... Gone with the Wind my brain flew, and over the cuckoo's nest, around the world in eighty milliseconds and back again before I even missed it. I really went back to that balance thing, didn't I? A last ditch effort before the bombs start flying overhead. And you were really enjoying this one? Shows what you know! Yes, there are two sides to every coin, and therefore, when the Indians sold Manhattan for $24 dollars, they got a great deal. What would they do with all that concrete anyway? Well, I think I'll put this baby to rest, and do the world, as well as my wrist, a tremendous favor. Until next time, sports fans. Keep the faith and keep the change.

♥   ♥   ♥

! No, that's not a typo. That is an

honest to goodness exclamation point. A noble punctuation mark, indeed. And it best describes my current state: There is an underlying excitement to every moment; a peaceful, easy feeling of connection and synchronicity, cradled in the arms of Spirit. I feel *the universe is putting on a show written by my thots, starring a cast of thousands of fellow travelers, and directed by God.* I can feel Innate tugging on my sleeve, saying, "Come on, you don't know how long I've waited for this!" Opportunities lurk behind every tick of the clock. My life is again beginning to look a lot more like my dreams...

I can see a progression in punctuation, across my adult life. Initially it was like a "colon": Sh-tty.

Then for a long time it was the age of the "comma," marking time, pausing, experimenting, basically seeing how many different chemicals my liver could detoxify (liver, a pretty-amazing organ, thank God). Something waited on the other side of the comma, but damned if I knew what it was.

It turned out to be chiropractic. *Thru chiropractic I caught a glimpse of the truth.*

Then I entered into the "question mark" era. My brain wanted answers to things it never previously even questioned. I wasn't ready for a lot of the answers I received. *The answers I was ready for, only birthed additional questions.*

Many layers around my heart began melting, and my seeking and questioning stirred up my passion for life, and for the discovery and the expression of my gifts. *Thru* the discipline I developed in my meditation and my other spiritual work, I found large pieces of my Self.

Which led to the "period" period. As I had "evolved spiritually" my ego found something new to sink its teeth into. I knew it all. There was nothing else to seek. I needed no one and nothing. I didn't need to hear anything or read anything. This cosmic arrogance somehow didn't stop the universe from continuing to work me.

My journey *brot* me to a "semi-colon;" broken in mid-run-on and half sh-tty. The half when I was still in my head, still attempting to run the show.

!!!!!!!! Man! It feels great to type that. Exclamation points bring up awe and adventure and passion and letting go and joy and freedom —everything I want in my life, and everything that is beginning to manifest.

Chiropractic should always be written with an exclamation point after it. The principle of chiropractic is a masterpiece of *thot*, a road map for self-discovery and self-expression, an incredibly *impact-full* idea! Numerous people healed *during my introductory talk* lately! And the chiropractic adjustment is

As I work that principle, it lovingly and perfectly works me!

a living, loving expression of the principle, changing lives wherever it goes. Such a deal! *As I work that principle, it lovingly and perfectly works me!* **!!!!!!!!!!!!!!!!!!!!!!!!**

Maybe my next book will be nothing but exclamation points. There may be a limited market, but just think of the fun?

♥ ♥ ♥

BE MY VALENTINE

Chiropractic, would you be my valentine? I do love you so, and I really think you love me, too.

You have showered me with gifts, and have graciously taught me to share mine. You have shown me miracles and whispered sweet everythings in my ear, and from you I have learned innumerable truths about myself, and about my Self.

Without words your song has reached deep into my heart and laid it open, and the Universe continues to open to me.

Your principle has ignited a divine spark that never was quite reached before with science or money or recreational drugs, and the world and I continue to benefit from the passion that has been unleashed.

Your simple and natural beauty has filled me with awe and continually reminds me of the incredible power I hold in my hands, and your magic continues to work thru them.

Your other servants have become my closest friends and dearest family, and I continue to glow with hope and optimism as I meet more and more of your warriors.

Best of all, you have never let me down, even when I've forsaken you by using you in name only, and you have helped me to develop a real relationship with God.

Be my valentine, chiropractic, and I vow to serve you, to love you, to protect you, to share you, to live you, and to be you.

On Valentines Day, know that I will be serving God by serving you. It's the most loving thing I know how to do. Even better, know that I'll be doing it the next day as well.

Dr. Stew Bittman

I've always *loved* Thanksgiving. I am filled with memories of Thanksgivings past that set me aglow with nostalgia and warm fuzzies.

Every year, or so it seemed, I ran upstairs into my cousin's bedroom to watch my favorite movie, *The March of the Wooden Soldiers*, and ritually march back and forth along with them. The music still brings a tear. Later years found me still running up to the same bedroom—by this time I had discovered my cousin's chocolate stash—now to watch something more in tune with my developing hormones.

Football! I can vividly remember Clint Longley, a quarterback no one ever heard of before or since, coming in after an injury to Roger Staubach, the starting quarterback, and throwing about a 200 yard TD pass in the closing seconds to win the game for the Dallas Cowboys.

Then of course there was the Thanksgiving meal, in all its tryptophan and starch-ridden glory. I generally arrived already half stuffed from my cousin's chocolate. In those days of my "chubbiness," as it was politely called, the meal was heaven.

But best of all, *tho* my family never adopted the conscious ceremony—and would invariably overeat, over-drink, belch, fart, and snore in the true American tradition—I could always detect a feeling, a warmth, a connection, before the belching and farting stage, of course, that was never present to the same degree at any other family functions. It felt so good to bask in the safe and nurturing energy of family. On Thanksgiving the beauty and the meaning of family entered a much deeper realm for all of us.

As this Thanksgiving approaches I am blessed to report I now experience that feeling more than once a year. That feeling of safety and connected-ness, of being part of something joyous and meaningful, of unconditional and unlimited support and love, is now a companion that never leaves me completely, even when I forget its presence. *I rest in the knowing that the world is my home, and that I am at home in the world.* And *tho* I rarely get together with my childhood family anymore on Thanksgiving, that feeling still connects us and binds us in tendrils of love.

Over the years I explored my Self, my Innate, and I allowed my heart to open. My family has grown to now include chiropractic folks all over the world. They are an integral part of my feeling of "belonging." A day never passes without at least a momentary awareness of our connection. Usually it is much more. When I am speaking, writing, adjusting, communing with nature, meditating, or whatever, they are often with me. I know on some level, every particle of matter in me knows exactly what every particle of matter in them is doing, and vice versa. More importantly, I know that our Innates are constantly dancing together, and will always be. Knowing these things keeps me keepin' on. And I am immensely grateful.

My chiropractic family is somewhere near the very top of the list

I rest in the knowing that the world is my home, and that I am at home in the world.

We are all interwoven in this magnificent tapestry called life. We are all on the same journey.

of innumerable gifts manifested in my life because of chiropractic. Some of them were there for every step on my journey, and they know me better at times than I know myself. With some I rubbed elbows and tushies while adjusting in Panama or Costa Rica or the Dominican Republic. We shared the miracle of chiropractic in its purest form. Others I met at seminars and workshops, and together we became inspired and empowered, and evolved and grew. Some of them I have not yet met in the flesh, yet we are still tightly and inextricably connected—that includes everyone —even those of you who aren't involved in chiropractic. *We are all interwoven in this magnificent tapestry called life. We are all on the same journey.*

On Thanksgiving, as I endeavor to buck the true American tradition —or at least to not explode, please know that I will also be sending love to you, and thanking God for the privilege of walking with you all on this glorious path.

♥   ♥   ♥

Just came in from shoveling six or seven inches of snow. This is April 17th, and yes, two days ago it was 70 degrees! It's Tahoe. The snow is falling like rain caught out in the cold and trying to return quickly to the warmth of Mother Earth. While I was out shoveling, I reflected with amusement about the complaints I will undoubtedly hear later concerning dead daffodils and buried golf courses, and "I *thot* it was spring!" I reached a further realization of The Great Mystery: Man, we really have no idea what's going to happen

My gifts are not about changing—they are about awakening. They create space for others to make their own changes. They are about love.

I didn't adjust the person to change them; I adjusted the person to help them connect to and express what is already inside.

I don't teach people about the chiropractic principle to change their belief system; I teach to help them remember who they are.

next, do we?

Of course, that doesn't stop us from trying to predict, to categorize, to even think we control. Yet, we are essentially clueless as we hurtle *thru* space, somehow hanging on to this spinning orb we call home. The unfathomable conspiracy that allows us to live our lives proceeds in our behalf, and I feel very humble when I consider the countless factors involved that are *all* maintained in balance.

Being at the ocean this past weekend was a further lesson in humility. I pondered the number of grains of sand on the beach. I felt the awesome majesty of the sea. I gazed in wonder at the whale spouts, and saw the teeming abundance of life in the smallest tide pool. Humble indeed. And humility is a state of grace.

I have found tremendous peace in the Great Mystery. A peace that I was never able to find in "the world"—even the world I worked so hard to manufacture to my specifications. After many years of being as good as anyone at trying to make sense of things, I now simply open my heart to all that is, and the perfection it represents. Even the things I don't like, and the things I wish would change.

People ask me where chiropractic fits in. If everything is perfect, why chiropractic? Why the need to change things, people, belief systems, attitudes, symptoms, or anything for that matter? Even the apparent unconsciousness that now pervades the planet, isn't that part of the plan? Here's my response:

Yes, it's perfect now, AND when chiropractic steps up and assumes its rightful place. When the world is aware and freer of interference, when the world is expressing more ease and more harmony and more spirit, it will STILL be perfect. There's a reason I was given the gifts I possess. My gifts are not about changing —they are about awakening. They create space for others to make their own changes. They are about love. When I adjust someone with love, with no attachments or expectations or desires, the universe quivers in joy, because it can then express and experience its essential nature with less interference. I didn't adjust the person to change them; I adjusted the person to help them connect to and express what is already inside. I don't teach people about the chiropractic principle to change their belief system; I teach to help them remember who they are.

I have even surrendered my need to figure out why subluxations exist. Those are misaligned bones in the spine that create interference to Innate's expression, and which chiropractors correct. If Innate can coordinate 600,000,000,000,000,000,000,000 things all at the same time, why can't it correct all subluxations? My brain can supply lots of ideas. I just know

To serve I must start where I am, and I must use my gifts.

With every breath, with every adjustment and with every moment to which I am fully present, I know more about joy and peace.

Every day I reach deep inside and glow and grow with the light that I find there within me.

subluxations exist. And whether they arise from slips, from stress, from fear, or from an Innate attempt to adapt or protect, I know that I have been put on this planet to minimize them and to maximize the flow of life. I recognize the perfection within the person, I connect to it, and I see nothing else except what is blocking its fullest manifestation. I am a gofer for Innate. A servant. And *to serve I must start where I am, and I must use my gifts.* I will never know if God wants subluxations corrected. I will never know the impact of my gifts on this planet. I will never know *that* Great Mystery.

Right now I am filled with certainty. Will I ever be completely free of doubts? Will I ever really know the importance of what I do? Who knows? I suppose not. But *with every breath, with every adjustment and with every moment to which I am fully present, I know more about joy and peace.* That's OK with me.

Every day I reach deep inside and glow and grow with the light that I find there within me. Every day I connect more and more to that light. Every day I remember more and more that the light is there, that it's me, and that it's the folk on my adjusting table, too. From that light, from that fundamental place within me, I can express certainty, faith, wisdom and love, and raise my consciousness above the level of the paradoxes. From that light I can express who I am and simply love and serve. If it is part of the plan for me to have a positive impact on the world it will come from the light within.

I am Innate. I am a child of God. I am love and service. Whatever I believe, conceive and achieve are all simply branches I send out in love, nourished by the sunlight and rain of the Creator. My branches grow out and intermingle with all others, and a tangle of love is created that encircles the planet. It's a heaven of a plan! And my part in it is perhaps infinitesimally small, but also infinitely indispensable. Wow.

And now for one final touch of seriousness:

Chiropractic is my life. It is my mission. My path to serve. Its principle is my road map for life. Its practice is my purest way to express love. *Thru* chiropractic I have experienced Innate, my connection to God. I have witnessed "miracles" which were simply Universal Intelligence expressing Itself from above down and inside out. I have seen lives changed, hearts opened, prayers answered, bodies and minds healed, simply *thru* the act of releasing the Law of life within. *Thru* chiropractic, I have become a shepherd. A steward. A warrior. A servant.

The word "universe" means one song. You can't alter a bar or a note without affecting the whole deal.

Picture a world in which all individuals are manifesting their plans, fulfilling their purposes, serving all others with their unique gifts and talents?

I have a large vision for what chiropractors do. By allowing Innate to express with less interference, we help reconnect the spirit and the flesh. We help reacquaint that individual with the Source of all his or her good and allow the greatest doctor in the Universe, who specializes in that individual, to do His works. With each adjustment delivered with that little something extra—love—we restore a bit more balance and harmony in the universe. *The word "universe" means one song. You can't alter a bar or a note without affecting the whole deal.* Chiropractic can help make the song a little sweeter. It can help smooth out some sour notes. Or tune some loose strings.

Each person or dog or whoever comes into my office is a unique expression of God. A personification (or dogification) of God. That individual's body is essentially an assortment of subatomic particles arranged into recycled atoms that are reorganizing themselves so fast you can't even see it. Somehow this mass of Twinkie and brown rice atoms is capable of doing quadrillions of things simultaneously

—including healing itself. There is a design for that individual. A plan. And I don't know the plan and I can't improve on the plan. But I can remove interference so that the plan can manifest. Isn't that beautiful?

Can you *picture a world in which all individuals are manifesting their plans, fulfilling their purposes, serving all others with their unique gifts and talents?*

Can chiropractic help change the world? Perhaps this brings up a little fear, or maybe a lot. Perhaps it brings up doubt, or even laughter. Perhaps it brings up your breakfast. It really doesn't matter. But if it resonates with you or ignites a spark in your consciousness, then take heart. I've seen the possibilities in Panama. Four times. I've seen the entire energy of a country change in six days. I've seen people line up by the thousands, wait for hours, walk for miles, carry people, and hand over their babies for a chiropractic adjustment. *I've experienced Innate working thru me to the exact extent that I could get myself out of the way.* It was easy to do in Panama, which allowed me to adjust 2000 people in a day, some of whom I never even physically touched. I've gained the knowledge of how powerful chiropractic can be when I use chiropractic in its purest form, and deliver it without any strings attached. Miracles inevitably result.

These same possibilities exist, not only in Panama, but everywhere.

Chiropractic is all about possibilities. And hope.

I hope you check it out.

♥   ♥   ♥

*I've
experienced
Innate working
thru me to the
exact extent
that I could get
myself out of
the way.*

*Chiropractic
is all about
possibilities.
And hope.*

Chapter 7:

Be or Do?

*"Believe me, you have to get up early
if you want to get out of bed."*
Groucho Marx

Writing for me is an excursion *thru* yet another apparent paradox, the one about being and doing. Sure, you've heard about that one for years, and you're pretty darned sick of it, too. *Do be do be do...*

After six and one-half innings, it's the Do(s) over the Be(s), 3-2. So take advantage of this seventh inning stretch and deal with it one more time.

Sometimes it's very clear which one is ahead. In Hawaii, for instance, "being" prevails. Even when I intend on doing something, like writing, the sun and the trade winds and the pace and the energy melt me into a state of Jello-ness. I don't think I could ever live there and do anything constructive again—OK, maybe I could handle a month or two.

The call to do, to create, to contribute, is too strong for me. The call to share my gifts is like the Siren's call.

On the other hand, *I'm not sure you can do or be one without the other.*

When I'm in Hawaii I'm still thinking, albeit on a more *aloha* level. And it's definitely possible to *do* while *being*. I've experienced that on several occasions. Like doing chiropractic missions in Panama, where I felt a connection to Innate that was seamless and real. I felt and allowed Its power to come *thru* my hands and my heart. Love was on the job. Mind, body and spirit all clocked in together.

I'm not sure you can do or be one without the other.

I was *doing*, but it wasn't me.

So maybe that doesn't count?

Judges, can we get your help with this? It counts, you say? Thank you.

That's 3-3, bottom of the 8th.

Come to think of it (another bizarre expression), all my most magical moments were similar, and the doing part in each case was effortless.

Writing is a perfect example.

My intention is always to allow my heart to flow onto these pages, and I feel that often happens. At other times, however, my heart is bottled up and I feel as if not a single word from me would ever interest anyone. The simple action of sitting at my desk and pecking away for a while often works as a corkscrew for my heart and a plug for my brain. It is then much more possible for me to express myself onto paper.

My pen floats over the page like a dipper over a rushing stream. Whirring and belting out its bold, wren-like song. It lets us all know it's there: I'm letting you know I'm here! But I promise my number one rule will continue to be: NO THINKING, ESPECIALLY WHEN WRITING. First *thots* directly from Innate to paper—The Paper Express—special delivery, hot off the press, unedited and unfiltered. Present moment stuff from the Master. That way I blend being and doing.

Are you listening?

Here goes:

A flower blooms somewhere and no one's there—does it sigh?

Oh how I wishigan that I was in Michigan, but Carolina is finer.

Or so they say in the redwoods where the fern is mightier than the sword or the chainsaw.

Oh, pardon me, does your underwear bunch up like that regularly, or is it an optical illusion?

Can you please examine your entrails somewhere else? There are children present and we don't want them growing up to be chiropractors now, do we?

Yesterday the sun belched and a giant rainbow arched across the back seat of a Greyhound bus rolling down Highway 41.

The cops chased the bus hither and yon, only

Why hold back?

Why not open myself completely?

Why not do in order to be more of a servant?

Why not surrender completely and just love?

Why not allow the acknowledged Master to run it all?

Innate rules!

to find Gideon's Bible.

We all prayed for deliverance and were very surprised to find out that the video store didn't carry it.

So we hopped on board and rolled off into the amber dawn of yesterday's tomorrow. Onward and upward we climbed, never realizing that all is well in the gunnysack of God.

Crap is what you'll often find in my writing, and yes, I am full of crap. But it's my crap, and it's full of life, and it's mostly first *thots* so bear with it.

Why hold back?

Why not open myself completely?

Why not do in order to be more of a servant?

Why not surrender completely and just love?

Why not allow the acknowledged Master to run it all?

Why not become so open that my brain and spleen and especially my heart are on my collar or sleeve or whatever I happen to be wearing? So open you can see my tonsils *thru* my ears!

Sounds good!

So I won't let the pen stop. Don't let it stop. Every drop is sacred. Every sperm, every egg, every rock, tree, lake, amoebae, person. All Innate. All God.

Write me, baby, 8-to-the-bar!

Write me like a wave rocks a ship to the lullaby of the moaning winds. Write me to awakening, so I can listen to the sweet siren song of Innate that never leaves me crashing on the rocks of desperation over the world's events, stories and dramas. Write me to the Promised Land of my heart, that holds the dreams I choose to manifest into this dream state I call my life.

Yes, by writing I am opening the sacred halls of me. Clearing the dust and cobwebs. Composting the crap, I turn it all over and the released gasses fuel my creativity. I can explore the darker corners hiding the darker secrets I've been unwilling to examine. There are some in there that would shock a few Quakers right out of their oatmeal! Others would put a slight blush on the Roseola Society. Still others might tickle the fancy of Smucker's Grape Preserves.

I know what you're thinking.

But it's my brain and I'll cry if I want to, cry if I want to, cry if I want to…

The *Schmootz Brigade* holds the key to the vault that contains all the meaningful emotional secrets that would belie its own illusory nature.

Unwilling to give up secrets, it sits there all puffed up with self-importance like a prison guard on a power trip. But in truth it is rather wimpy and has no power whatsoever outside of the artificial rules of the game that it invented. So I'll just play by different rules… Innate's rules.

Oh, to be in the flow of God's Love in every moment. To be in the flow of Mother Earth when She declares Her ecstasy thru creating all this beauty.

Innate rules!

Bang the cymbals and shake the tambourines and stop the presses because another soul is emerging. My vault is being cleaned by God's janitorial service. Come on in boys, the walls are a bit dusty with *crapola*, but you can start right in on that brain—it's that large thing up above. Yes, steam clean that thing and don't forget to iron out some of those wrinkles. We've got to have things Spic'n'Span as we're going on strike against the cerebral hemispheres. We're holding out for more pay and shorter hours. They'll only back us until the first sign of trouble. Then they'll sell us out so fast our little limbic systems will spin around three times and land on "Go," at which time we'll have to sell our hotels and move to Park Place—if they haven't torn it down to build a new Wal-Mart.

Why not be the source of magic in my life? Why not be the sorcerer's apprentice and co-create the magical, benign being I would love to be? Why not decipher the code of existence with the key of Love? Why not be a paragon of being and condemn nothing but my own self-pity and *thots* of lack and separation? Why not stand and be in my power? To hell with the *Schmootz Brigade!* This is my highest choice! I banish you AGAIN *Schmootz Brigade!* Go lick bootstraps in the artillery of Genghis Khan. Go have a wonderful time salivating over the lessons you've prevented me from learning. Don't you see you're just a cream pie waiting to be thrown in the face of my spirit? Can't you understand that love is the answer to all the rhetoric that comes out of your mouth?

Oh, to be in the flow of God's Love in every moment. To be in the flow of Mother Earth when She declares Her ecstasy thru creating all this beauty.

God, do you really care what I say and write and do, or are you out there creating planets and galaxies and not to be bothered? Are you really watching over us or watching old reruns of *Ozzie and Harriet*? Did you split in the 60's right after *Dragnet* came out? Or are *You* responsible for all the crap we've got nowadays? Sorry about that—no offence I hope.

This pen is really cooking now. It's almost keeping up with my mind. Even wings can't fly higher. Only Spirit can soar over the rainbow to the *vas deferens* of time.

Why don't we do it in the road? Or at least under the boardwalk where the moon comes to tea wearing nothing but a grin? Don't you know that buttons are meant to pop off when the time is right for dancing in the streets?

What a tragedy was just averted! My cat just jumped into my lap and almost knocked my coffee all over these pages. These pages hold the key to my heart.

But the key is rusty and the chains are so thick.
A blowtorch might be more helpful,
But it's got quite a kick.
Unchain my heart, but don't fry my gizzard!
Be gentle. Be loving. Be kind.
Be like Mikey. He likes it. He loves it!
But don't bother asking him why.
He won't be able to say, but he may
Spit his cereal across the room,
Which is always entertaining.

There are no answers. Only ideas. There are so many ideas that the Universe is getting crowded. There must be a plug around here some-where to let some ideas out. It's filling up fast, so if you plan on having any ideas you'll have to wait 'til February when we have an opening.

You see that beige wall over there on Park Place? We must climb it in order to pass Go and collect $200. Then we can ponder

There's nothing more precious than this day and this moment.

Whenever I've done something with an intention to share my heart and have really been present, I was integrating being and doing. It is the ultimate balancing act, and the key to changing the world, for that's where Love is found.

the right moment to pounce on the lily pad. If the frog fits, shoe it.

Why do you frown so? Because you don't get it?

Well, let me tell you this. By the time you get it, it will already have left. Its meter is running and it doesn't have time to wait around for all of us to finish our tea and join the foxhunt. So get on with it.

OK, I will.

Life, I love you. I salute the dawn with my chin held high, my upper lip stiffened, and my guns emptied. I embrace you, Thursday; you are my gift. A gift from God, with which I can do or be in any combination imaginable. *There's nothing more precious than this day and this moment,* so why am I wasting time talking to You? Just kidding again, God.

Where were we? Oh, yes—*being* and *doing.*

I suppose that *whenever I've done something with an intention to share my heart and have really been present, I was integrating being and doing. It is the ultimate balancing act, and the key to changing the world, for that's where Love is found.*

Another Panama mission has recently come and gone, and even *tho* we chose not to participate in this one, I could feel the energy of it. All week during the mission, I could feel the excitement and the joy and the miracles, as well as the inevitable (albeit very few) hassles and frustrations and ego conflicts. I could feel the unconditional love being given and received. I could feel hearts opening to new realms of possibilities.

How much more value is there in an experience if we stay diligent to the possibilities revealed thru it, and continue to do the work that opens the door to Grace?

As a servant and a warrior, I need to be in the world—not necessarily of the world, but in it.

Only by being in the world can I become a true servant. Only by being in the world can I rise above it.

I could even feel the heat! And now I can feel the energy of chiropractors returned to their offices, attempting to bring the love and energy of their recent experiences back into their everyday practices and lives. The hard part, for sure.

The experience of a Panama mission is indescribable. Witnessing the incredible power and simplicity of the chiropractic principle and art, delivered with no strings attached to the love and service, and depending completely on the power of Innate to take over on both ends of the adjustment, is an amazing gift, indeed. It is an experience of love and unlimited possibilities; an experience that carries a huge surge of the energy of awakening to its participants, to a nation, and to the world. It is an experience of incredible value.

I wonder how much more value could that experience manifest, when we as chiropractors unleash the gift of it here, in our own practices and our own communities?

How much more value is there in an experience if we use it to further our growth and our ability to serve?

How much more value is there in an experience if we remember to use it as a bellows to fan the fire of our passion?

How much more value is there in an experience if we stay diligent to the possibilities revealed thru it, and continue to do the work that opens the door to Grace?

Even an experience that brings healing and hope to hundreds of thousands of people, as happens in Panama, can be magnified infinitely when it is integrated into one's very being—when a heart remains open and continues to serve without strings.

Indeed, how much more value is there in any experience, if we don't separate it from the rest of our lives?

I am confident that we all have amazing spiritual experiences. Often I find myself desiring to sit on a beach in Hawaii communing with the magnificent creations of Mother Earth, or to hide in a cave in the Himalayas in constant meditation and prayer for the world. There is tremendous value in such experiences, for myself and for all of creation. Yet, *as a servant and a warrior, I need to be in the world—not necessarily of the world, but in it.*

In a cave or on a beach or in Panama, it is easy for me to know that God is with me, and that God is working *thru* me. It is easy to know my connection to everything—easy for me to know my essence and to allow that essence to erupt from deep within me.

In the world, my knowledge of those things is tested —big time. Only by being in the world, *thru* my relationships and *thru* my service to others, can I find: Where I am blocking that flow; How I fall back into my illusion of separateness; and What I have not

When Innate and I are one, there is no interference between my heart and my head; not only is everything perfect, but it is enough.

"When is enough actually enough?"

Whenever I looked to the outside... I never experienced enough.

learned to love about myself! *Only by being in the world can I become a true servant. Only by being in the world can I rise above it.*

Upon returning from Panama, many experience what I call the "post-Panama blues"—including me. Back in the "real world," the Panama experience or any other experience of being used by God can seem unattainable. The only cure for the post-Panama blues is to keep my heart wide open. Let the experience flood my heart, let it saturate my consciousness, and let it emerge from every pore. Let it stand as a beacon, toward which my path continually winds. Let it fuel my warrior engine.

As I do those things, I can see a world with much more health, sanity, joy, abundance, principle, and spirit. It begins in our own hearts, in our own lives, and *thru* our own experiences.

The crowds are assembling in Stateline, Nevada, here at Lake Tahoe, preparing for another New Year's Eve of reveling, drinking and freezing their behinds off—celebrating God knows what. This is considered "the thing to do" in these parts. I'm sure at one time in my life I would have been another rowdy and frozen behind in the crowd, wondering the next morning, "why on earth did I...?"

It's funny how things that seem important change.

This becomes rather evident when I look over past lists of New Year's resolutions. These lists, cluttered with all the things I wanted to have, wanted to do, and wanted to be, now make me either shake my head, cringe, or gag. Thus they provide a crystal clear road map to where my happiness really lies—Innate.

When Innate and I are one, there is no interference between my heart and my head; not only is everything perfect, but it is enough.

A critical question is, *"When is enough actually enough?"* Man, I can relate... *Whenever I looked to the outside,* which is where I looked most of my life, *I never experienced enough.*

There was never enough! Regardless of how many folks I adjusted; how many trips I took or talks I gave; how many miracles I witnessed; how many thank you notes and warm wishes I received; how many hours of meditation I logged; how much energy I expended; or how much approval I elicited. It was never enough.

Often now I look for and find enough in the face of one baby. The feel of a breeze. A sunset. I experience enough when adjusting or hiking or golfing or doing the dishes or filling out a report—well OK, I would if I actually ever did file a report. As long as I am fully present it is enough. I bask in enough when I am with my family and good friends, doing nothing.

I am finally learning *my brain can NEVER know enough, and my heart knows nothing else.*

Enough is good enough for me.

So my resolution list is short this year. I still have my goals and intentions as a road map for my dreams, and I know they will not bring me enough, whether I actually reach them or not.

To have a mission and live it is enough.

To be a servant is enough.

To learn and grow is enough.

To give and receive love is enough.

To open my heart and reside there is enough.

To help one person open their heart is enough.

To be a child of God is enough.

Man, when you look at the word "enough" enough, it sure starts to look wrong!

Here's to a year with an abundance of enough-ness, overflowing with all the miracles that come *thru* these beautiful vehicles called bodies and minds.

Happy New Year!

My brain can NEVER know enough, and my heart knows nothing else.

To give and receive love is enough.

To open my heart and reside there is enough.

Chapter 8:

Strive or Surrender?

"Clear? Huh! Why, a four-year-old
child could understand this report.
Run out and find me a four-year-old child.
I can't make head or tail out of it."
Groucho Marx

I once made the statement, "I surrender everything to God, but I still like to check up on Him every once in a while." I said it in jest, or so I *thot*. Now that I think about it, it was true. It afforded me the luxury of giving up responsibility for my choices, and at the same time, of having someone else to blame when things seemingly went awry.

Yes indeed, I could talk a good game, but I didn't believe it. I had concepts in my head that sounded good and even rang of truth; but without *evidence* I had no *feeling*, and without feeling I had no knowing, and without *knowing* none of it got past my filters to Innate.

What I did have, even back then, was an *intention*

to find out. To explore my boundaries in order to discover if those boundaries were valid or simply created and placed there by me. To dive headfirst into the spiritual life. To dedicate myself to practice and discipline. To bring the tools I learned along the way into my everyday life. *To be willing to march into the hell of losing self for the heavenly cause of finding Self.*

Thru that process I have accumulated lots of evidence. And here I am: still finding out, still exploring, still diving, still willing, still learning... but way-way freer, much more peaceful and more aware. Still surrendering, and still checking up once in a while, but way less.

This weekend I was "supposed to be" in Las Vegas, attending a well-known chiropractic seminar. I really wanted to go. A lot. My best friends were going to be there. I haven't attended in two years, but I've been to 25 of them, and I have a lot of old friends I looked forward to seeing. I was pretty sure I would have an opportunity to speak, and possibly even establish a regular speaking venue there. I was even excited about the idea of sleeping

Be willing to march into the hell of losing self for the heavenly cause of finding Self.

in my own room, all by myself, something I don't get to do very often. *Tho* Hillary was pretty sick, I convinced myself she would be fine at home. I felt a cold or something coming on, but I figured I can have a cold anywhere. The overnight forecast called for a snowstorm, but what else is new at Tahoe? In other words, my ego was having a picnic and it wasn't about to let the red ants of reason ruin its plans.

Mother Nature was indeed busy overnight, depositing a foot and a half of snow, and she showed no signs of taking a breather. The wind was blowing the snow out of the trees, creating zero-visibility whiteouts. I awoke at six am Thursday, planning to leave at 7:30, and as I was shoveling out, doubts were creeping in.

"What are you, nuts?" Innate insisted.

"I've got 4-wheel drive, and I drive in this stuff all the time," I offered with ever-diminishing enthusiasm.

"You're going to leave your family to deal with this alone?" Innate countered, sounding very much like my mother.

"Hmmm," was about the best thing I could muster.

Hillary didn't help at all. She feigned she would indeed "be fine," but she worried about me driving. "Why don't you meditate on it," she said, sounding very much like Innate.

I did. I sat for about 10 minutes asking for *clarity*.

I opened my eyes and was disoriented for a moment, until I realized what I was seeing out the window was wind-blown snow. I could not even see the trees only five feet from the window! Clarity...

"When you give a sign, you don't fool around, do you?"

Well, I didn't go. I checked up a little bit. I felt sorry for myself a little bit. And then the phone rang.

It was my father-in-law. My mother-in-law recently had her drivers license revoked pending a hearing, and they have both been increasingly despondent. They chose this particular day to lose it completely.

Sounding as *tho* on his deathbed, he asked if we could come over. Now I was really pissed.

"Not only do I *not* get to go to Las Vegas, but I have to deal with this! My neck hurts and my head is pounding. They're acting like babies. They think they've got the future all figured out, and they can't see the possibility of anything good coming of this," I raged.

A faint voice cried, "Remember all those tools you've learned." Maybe it was Hillary. I remembered to breathe. I remembered my ongoing intention: *don't let expectations or past events mar your present moment experience.*

In the silence Innate boomed, "You make me sick. And I can't even GET sick. Haven't you been asking to serve? Didn't you state

Don't let expectations or past events mar your present moment experience.

an intention to stick around home more? Isn't it you that preaches to everyone else that everything is perfect, that only Spirit knows the big picture, and that loving acceptance of the present moment is the key to a peaceful life? Don't you realize YOU manifested all of this, and aren't you doing exactly what you're accusing your in-laws of doing?"

"Ah, shut up already," I muttered, sounding very much like my in-laws.

Off we went.

On the way, Hillary thanked me and admitted there was no way she could have physically gotten herself *thru* the snow to help her folks, nor could she have been emotionally able to deal with them alone.

I began to understand why I stayed home.

As the weekend progressed more of my attachments were tested, and more opportunities to serve presented themselves. A young man in our practice fell on the ice and cracked his head and shoulder. He was numb on his right side from head to toe. He called, hoping I hadn't left yet for Las Vegas. I was able to adjust him and watch him heal. I was able to adjust and otherwise tend to Hillary, as well as to the snow, to the cooking, to the in-laws and to the fire. And when my Innate launched Its full-scale adaptation to the virus that had gotten beyond my initial lines of defense—when the "crud" hit me—I was able to rest, ground myself and catch up on a bunch of stuff. I was able to focus on my *thots* and find clarity on a lot of things.

Best of all, I was able to learn another lesson about acceptance and surrender—and do it consciously.

I'm sure God doesn't mind that I check up on Him

now and then. She continues to create the space for me to manifest my highest good, just as She does for everyone, for all eternity, whether or not we choose to jump into that space. *God continues to smile upon all my lessons, whether or not I learn them, and continues to give, whether or not I turn my back on His gifts.* He continues to provide opportunity, abundant materials and infallible guidance. She continues to love me, without strings attached, whether or not I'm awake enough to know it. The Supreme Servant for sure. Having chosen to serve, I thank God I have such a magnificent example to follow.

God continues to smile upon all my lessons, whether or not I learn them, and continues to give, whether or not I turn my back on His gifts.

We never play popular music in the office. It is extremely rare, amongst the eclectic mix of Celtic and Native American and other assorted stuff we do play, to even hear a lyric. That's why it struck me as unusual to hear Hillary playing the Jerry Garcia Band in the office a few weeks ago. It was even more unusual to hear it being played off and on all day long. Then late in the afternoon, one of our younger folks came in, and it didn't strike me as nearly so odd to hear him ask if we were playing Jerry because it was the anniversary of his death. No, Hillary had no idea it was that particular date or even close to it, but I suppose Innate was on the job.

Yes, *what a long strange trip it's been*.

At one time, I would have dismissed such an event as coincidental; an isolated occurrence that my mind would quickly discard like an old sock that lost its mate and therefore its meaning in my life. If only they mated for life! I'm sure Innate was on the job back then, but my ego made sure I was eternally out to lunch. Then for a long while, after becoming aware of the possibility of another realm of existence, this kind of thing could not be dismissed as easily. Synchronicity would tug at the sleeve of my consciousness, begging for recognition and acceptance, trying to get me to acknowledge its place in the rest of my life. Ultimately, of course, it would fail. I might even go so far as to say to myself, "Sure would be nice if this One Mind and synchronicity stuff was on the level, but..." I would finally let it go as being too weird, too bizarre for my little brain that still wanted things *separate, labeled* and *logical*. Yes, Innate was on the job, and yet Ego was still not willing to give it full-time status or benefits.

Well, after years of whatever it is I've been doing, we're working on throwing a semi-retirement party for Ego. We'll heap praise upon it for a job well done, and then give Innate the key to the executive washroom of my awareness.

I surrender. My *life is one coincidence, one synchronistic event after another.* I no longer discard any pieces—much as I'd like to discard some of them!

This principle of chiropractic really does apply to every area of my life. It dances around and *thru* my flesh, my *thots*, my emotions, my spiritual awareness, my relationships, my career and my finances. It not only applies, it works! This uni-verse truly is one song, and the Supreme Composer, Conductor and Choreographer maintains all the notes in perfect connection and coordination. Coincidence is a brain function; Innate knows only connection—harmony. Logic is a brain function—Innate knows only wholeness. *Separation is a hallucination that Innate sees only as one-ness.*

The 32nd principle of chiropractic states, "Coordination is the principle of harmonious action of all the parts of an organism, in fulfilling their offices and purposes." This not only applies to the human organism, but also to the "organism" called the Universe. *We have,*

My life is one coincidence, one synchronistic event after another... what a long strange trip it's been.

Separation is a hallucination that Innate sees only as one-ness.

whenever we're ready to claim it, the unlimited ability to live our offices and purposes, with our actions always benefiting the other parts of the organism in cooperation and coordination. And just like a tissue cell in a harmonious body, all our needs will be met. Such a sweet deal.

If we apply this principle, Innate will then truly be on the job, and this world will become more of the beautiful song it is designed to be. Jerry Garcia used to sing, *"Oh, what I want to know, how does the song go?"* Well, I'm not sure if we need to know how it goes, but we certainly can dedicate our lives to getting our individual notes in tune. We can know those tuned notes fit perfectly in the song, and we can use our gifts to help others tune their notes. Happy tuning!

Put the pen on the paper and turn the nozzle on the faucet and drain the brain.

The brain drain game. It's sweeping the nation and the nation was surely getting pretty dusty. Order now and receive absolutely nothing, but get rid of lots of crapola that's holding you back. Become aware of yourself and your Hayley's M-O and learn to say no to your ego-self—that part of you that creates dung out of God's repository of loveliness. You know—the Schmootz Brigade that sits ready to pounce with thots of lack and limitation and weakness and separation. The Schmootz Brigade is very antisocial and likes no one including you. It must enjoy not liking you,

We have, whenever we're ready to claim it, the unlimited ability to live our offices and purposes, with our actions always benefiting the other parts of the organism in cooperation and coordination.

Go God and leave the driving to Him.

Our spirits soar toward knowing each other without disguise.

because it's always around to tell you how inadequate you are. It lurks in its den and froths at the mouth waiting for you to feed it live bits of your consciousness. Create a new you... call today!

A mind is interesting. It can soar, float, sink or swim with the best of them. Once in a while it can even glow like a firefly against the coal, black sky. Other times it grinds gears, like backing out of the driveway with the emergency brake on. I often have my emergency brake engaged—that's one of my problems. Let it go. Let it ride. Let it happen. Let it go, full speed ahead, and let the Great Spirit do the driving. *Go God and leave the driving to Him.* He can drive pretty well even *tho* He's simultaneously running an entire universe.

Dark, obliterating dark.
To the shores of your darkness
I paddle.
Ever wary of the light. It comes.

We dance it away to no avail.
It roars and reaches its fingers
Around the throat of darkness.
It squeezes its life to the next level
And lights the path.
All follow to the light,
A beacon for new thots and new ideas.
It brings a wash of color to the world,
And God smiles.

Hey, if it's drivel to you how do you think I feel? I wrote it. Or did I? Did I write it or did it write me?

What's really on my mind is how frisky I was feeling yesterday, and also the rollicking way my friskiness was abated. I love surrender. The tangle of loving bodies underscored a unique relationship between our hearts — we intertwined, alive with the sound of music. It's a thrill that is far from gone. Onward to new heights of ecstatic passion as *our spirits soar toward knowing each other without disguise*. We stand naked before one another and before God, with our souls exposed and our truths revealed. So lovely. So beautiful. So intimate. As our bodies embroil with the flow of Spirit's essence our minds relax in a hot tub of Love. We do our bidding without regard for strife or confusion as our energies combine to create a new state of synthesis and form. And it feels good, too. The change is gonna do you good. So line up and be the first on your block to experience this new sensation: Love.

Such is life in the big city of my existence. Maybe I should move to the suburbs, or the country, where I can dance with Fred Astaire and Ginger Rogers across the fields of lilies awash in the meadow. Does the meadow need to be *awashed?* If so it will probably soon *arain*.

And I bid you good night. Good night!

♥   ♥   ♥

AM I NUTS OR WHAT?

I find it easy to strive
To swim upstream
To proclaim good or bad
To analyze and judge

I find it easy to complain
To find the fault
To blame one and all
To give away my power

I find it easy to question
To figure things out
To attempt to control
To forever ask why

I find it easy to hate
To see the differences
To mistrust and doubt
To live in fear

I find it hard to surrender
To flow with the design
To experience and learn
To remember who I am

I find it hard to be thankful
To be in awe
To see the blessings
To bask in the Divine

I find it hard to let go
To let it all happen
To enjoy the ride
To let God handle it

I find it hard to remember
To live in joy
To love myself
And my brothers and sisters

AM I NUTS OR WHAT?

♥   ♥   ♥

\

Chapter 9:

We're All The Same;
Why Are We So Different?

"Love flies out the door when
money comes innuendo."
Groucho Marx

I slept in the back room last night. Hillary has been doing her no-sleep-around-the-full-moon thing. She finally resorted to an herbal sleeping pill. As she sits across from me at the dining room table this morning, I can only hope it worked. Well, she just reported that she slept beautifully from about 8:30 until 11 p.m., and then resumed her doze/wake/in-between cycle. Wow. I at least, can parade around with some energy today, since I was able to sleep more like a log than like a baby.

So today begins our first promotion of the year in our office. Our promotions are more like promotions this year, as suddenly I've been struck with this crazy notion that it's OK to ask for help, to promote for

If you adopt your natural abundance consciousness, you can sit in First Class and get a tablecloth on top of your tray table, too.

We are the same, playing life with the same dramas, with only minor variations in the cast and script.

Our lives are so intertwined that to consider them as separate is lunacy.

new "business," and even to have lots of money! Yes, can you believe it? The long-awaited OK-ness to be abundant and to actually have the things I want in their normal and natural bounteous state, has finally arrived.

And like a long train, it will take a while to pass.

Just kidding. I intend to remain on the train and to sit in First Class, and also to look the coach folks right in the eye to pass along the silent message: *If you adopt your natural abundance consciousness, you can sit in First Class and get a tablecloth on top of your tray table, too.* And we can sit together and sip Merlot and get a choice of ice cream sundaes and maybe we can share the hot fudge and the butterscotch. We can have it all… *tho* I suppose we would never know if we indeed had it all? These imaginations of ours keep coming up with more and more to have.

You and I are so alike. Of the quadrillions of things we share, not only as members of the same species, but also as creations of the Universal Mind, so few of those are different. And yet we focus on those differences! Indeed, we see only the differences, and those differences cause us to separate from each other and from everything else. This hallucination of *being different* causes suffering and war and all those other things that don't feel so good. And the simple fact is: *we are the same, playing life with the same dramas, with only minor variations in the cast and script. Our lives are so intertwined that to consider them as separate is lunacy;* and yet the world is full of lunatics, and we all indulge in the illusion to various degrees. Craziness!

Well, this crazy guy is wild with the deep knowing that craziness is something I conjured early in life, based on overwhelming crazy input. Now I practice daily the art of disconnecting from my brain so that I can observe the craziness and perhaps even get sane for a moment or two.

It seems nutty, but my mind so often berates me about my writing. Specifically, with its rather firm opinion that I have nothing to say and certainly don't say it as well as every other writer. It opines that I most assuredly have nothing new to say, and that I keep writing about the same things over and over.

Well, phooey on you, young man. So what!

It may smack of truth that there are several recurring themes in my writing, but to that I say, "Ha!" I can see you are impressed with the cleverness of my retort.

But really, these are the themes that my life and my intentions have centered around for years. By writing about them over and over, I am cutting/pasting/slashing and shedding and sculpting away at them. I know somewhere in there is the truth for me. Every time I write about them I come at them from a slightly different place. I've heard, "You can't walk in the same river twice." Even if you could, would it be so bad? Rivers are kind of wonderful to walk in. *Does every thing in life have a cosmic purpose?*

Back to the metaphor of the slashing/sculpting thing... *Thru* the process of writing *I am peeling away layers of mist that shroud the expression of my Innate wisdom;* clarity tends to emerge as the mist lifts (say 'mist lifts' five times fast!). I am honing it down, chipping and chiseling away at the extraneous droppings that accumulated — continually learning how to curb my dog so that maybe someday I can actually retire the pooper-scooper. Oh, what a beautiful morning that will be! Everything's coming my way, and writing helps me to open to exactly what I want to let in. I whittle away at the filters that keep me in this B-movie starring

Does every thing in life have a cosmic purpose?

I am peeling away layers of mist that shroud the expression of my Innate wisdom

separation and fear. I allow more and more of Innate's script to reveal itself.

But boy, the mind works fast. First *thots* flee like thieves in the night, chased by the sirens of Ego and its hordes of flak-jacketed thugs—like Judgment, Comparison, Doubt and the whole *Schmootz Brigade*. Yes, boys, I see you've returned from your latest banishment. Welcome home.

You know, it's like chiropractic. Why do people need to be adjusted over and over and over again? I know that's a commonly asked question, eliciting all kinds of answers, some of which beg the question at best. I love that expression "beg the question." I suppose, if you beg long enough you'll be thrown a scrap or a milk bone; other than your teeth being a little whiter, I'm not sure if you'll be really happy about it? But at least Ego won't go hungry. Anyway, I think people, myself included, require lifetime adjustments for the same reason I continue to write about the same subjects.

Michelangelo, who saw the finished sculpture in a lump of clay, simply needed to chisel away the rest. I have the same approach to chiropractic. I help chisel away everything that is not love and Innate. Of course, it didn't take Michelangelo a lifetime to get his job done, but he didn't have his subjects grabbing piles of clay that had been removed and sticking them back on! Man, do we get attached to our stuff!

Yes, indeedy, we do, and this makes the spiritual path, as well as chiropractic care, vitally essential to the servant's credo. Piles of excrement lie unfettered along the byways of our cortical neurons, and the shoveling and composting is a never-ending proposition, to which I am dedicated. Yes, and the one about all men being created equal is worth dedicating one's self to as well, as long as we realize, "that's right, the women are smarter."

Adjustments open the heart and allow the Innate cleaning crew to pick up the clay and the feces and dispose of it *thru* proper channels, most of which are not worth watching.

Speaking of that, the Super Bowl is today and my streak of *not watching* it seems safe. Hopefully, Iraq, or whoever, will not seize on the idea I got from Tom Robbins about invading on *this* national holiday, when everyone is especially *unconscious*, and most everyone is drunk with drink and violence and rah-rah-rah.

Opening the heart to the keyboard is what this is all about. Let's get my heart and this keyboard connected, so Innate can deliver the words direct to you without the middlemen getting their filthy hands on any of them (editors beware)! The Producer can get the product to you in 3-5 working days and you don't even have to pay COD. You can pay GOD if you want, but I think all She really wants from you is to stop playing Her. Then we all can spend our time flourishing and thriving and dancing and hopping and skipping and jumping our way *thru* the hoops of existence with smiles on our faces and ice cream all over the smiles. Yes, I imagine you didn't know the Ben and Jerry rule, but you have indeed led a sheltered life, haven't you? This all-critical principle simply states: Ice cream holds the key to happiness and you don't even have to eat it; you simply rub it all over your face. Actually, that's preferable.

So start rubbing and leave the driving to Greyhound. Or your wife. Pull over to the side of the road there and let's see your license to operate that brain of yours. Ah-ha! Just as I *thot*, you don't have one, do you? Well, come along with me and we'll see about applying for one, and then you'll be released with a warning about not operating your brain until the license arrives, which will be never, if you're lucky.

Re-reading several years of my journal pages taught me a few important lessons. Well, one anyway. As discussed earlier, and later, and all *thru*-out, I tend to think about the same issues and the same intentions. The pages from five or six years ago, assuming I can find them, will undoubtedly disclose the same stuff. So much stuff! And, as I mentioned earlier in the piece about pieces, there are so many pieces! Because the *Schmootz Brigade* is alive and well and spilling pieces of its guts all over the white linen tablecloths of my life, much of its gut-spilling comes out in my journalizing. Generally it's up front in the first page or two, and then Innate steps in with the love and the answers. The news from the front is so bad, we will all be moving to the rear—so move your rear and get in line. Yes, the *Schmootz Brigade* makes me cynical of everything that is part of my *raison d'être*.

The same issues and intentions return like relatives that I've treated too well over the years.

Why, *praytell*, does spell check accept *raison,* and not *d'être*? Or *praytell* for that matter? Maybe it's two words: pray tell. Yes, it liked that better. So, now I've managed to find another thing in the universe I live to seek approval from: spell check!

As I was saying before I was so rudely interrupted... *The same issues and intentions return like relatives that I've treated too well over the years*, bringing their whining, snotty nosed kids with them. And nothing ever seems to change, yet, you look around and nothing is the same. And on it goes, where she stops nobody knows. But that doesn't stop everyone from thinking they know exactly where it goes. It goes on the shelf right there, next to all that memorabilia from the campaign against cyclamates—you're probably too young to remember that, so put it in the garbage where it truly belongs.

As long as I don't exclusively rent the upstairs to the *Schmootz Brigade*, and I continue to love it and to remember my connection to Spirit, clarity always emerges like Excalibur from the misty lake. Why is it still so easy for the mists to reform around my intentions and my connection and my truth? My brain loves mist. It should move to Seattle. It can drink lots of Starbucks, get wired, and spend hours on its favorite activities like creating molehills out of mountains. Then it can climb up the Space Needle and sow some really wild oats before leaping to its doom. Knowing my brain and how well it's been trained to look before it leaps, I guess that won't work. But something in me is surely smiling at the possibility!

I've been writing with this same expensive pen for months and it has more lives than a passel of cats. Or is it a Cassel of pats? Or a castle of Pats? Can you imagine? One Pat is enough for most situations so I guess a castle of Pats would be enough for a castle of situations.

There are two small hairs on this page and I wonder from where they came? Yes, they came from God, but where have they been hanging out since then? Were they created to be bookmarks for this page, indicating something really hairy is ready to emerge upon it?

Who cares whether he or she is right? Everyone, unfortunately! It's perhaps the single greatest illusion in our society.

My truth is only a facet of the Truth, just as my Innate is like a cupful of the ocean of God.

We're all spinning around the hub of God like spokes on a magnificent wheel, holding true in orbit around our divine center.

Well, I removed the offending hairs and threw them on the floor, thus once again demonstrating another thing I yell at Ari about. I even yelled at her in my dream last night:

I was supposed to be having some kind of private meeting attended by hundreds of people, including Ari and Hillary. Ari kept interrupting me and kept proclaiming she was right, and I was irate with her right there in my dream. Indeed, that's the button you push for me oh so well, Ari: BEING RIGHT.

Who cares whether he or she is right? Everyone, unfortunately! It's perhaps the single greatest illusion in our society. The one that makes for more hatred and judgment and separation than anything else. I'm right and you're Catholic and you're black and you're gay and you're Republican and you're stupid, and you're exactly like me.

My truth is only a facet of the Truth, just as my Innate is like a cupful of the ocean of God. So my cup of truth is no different or more right than yours—we just need to click our cups together as we toast to the idea that somewhere in all these cups is the Truth. We might examine these other cups without too much attachment to our own and see which pieces of the Truth are contained therein.

We are so much alike, all of us. All a little nuts, with slightly different ways of showing it. And hiding it.

We're all spinning around the hub of God like spokes on a magnificent wheel, holding true in orbit around our divine center. From the center I can be anything and everything I choose. My personality, my somebody-ness, my *Schmootz Brigade,* spin in time and space way out there around my Innate center, and I take turns identifying with different parts. My ego goes for countless rides on the merry-go-round, spinning around the circumference — probably why they call them ego trips — and every day I end up in a different spot from which to view myself and everything else. I need to constantly gather my centripetal forces by simply remembering; I move away from Center by simply forgetting. Out there on the periphery I am limited in vision, limited in power, limited in productivity, limited in everything. So I set a course for the center. The good news is the pull of gravity is strong and incessant. All return there, some consciously. I choose to consciously return, and then my occasional forays back to the periphery can be part of my daily experience of all that is. But home is home, and home is where the heart is. And the heart is where Innate is. And Innate is where God is. *I realize God by staying home, not by being right.*

The seas of logic part as I forge onward from my heart. I serve in the most productive, unattached way I can envision. I float *thru* the Universe on wings of Spirit and resist being Velcroed to the sides or the bottom—especially the bottom. I'm heading for the top but the top is always just the bottom of the next level. So I'm really on the Universal elevator! I've pushed the Self-button. And I'm heading in unknown directions down uncharted paths that are selected especially for me like the Newlywed Game. Wouldn't it be funny if the ultimate goal turned out to be a washer and dryer?

I realize God by staying home, not by being right.

This pen finally seems to be slowing down a bit, but is not yet dead, as I thot a few minutes ago. The rumors of its demise were greatly exaggerated and also prematurely ejaculated from my hand onto this page. Ignore them; they were simply released from some remote parts of my bean brain. There's a special today on bean brain chairs. You sit in them all day and do nothing but think, judge, analyze, doubt, and question everything of value while you contemplate the virtue of worldly possessions. We used to stock them, but we're clearing the decks for the storm of truth already blowing things around. My ego is rocking and rolling on its imaginary pedestal, and it's OK, because I'll throw it a peppermint lifesaver of love. So batten down the hatches, for the Castle of Pats is wavering in the breezes of reality.

AUTUMN CHANGES

Every change allows us to
reap the harvest
from all that has come before,
to flow with the timeless
ever-changing winds,
to surrender to the seamless plan,
and explore our boundaries.

In each moment there are no constants
of time or space,
only stitches in a Universal
fabric that unite and detach
in an eternal circle,
knowing no agendas.

As the Mother begins her period of rest and renewal,
we seek our own destinies,
gently, lovingly, and with heads held high,
allowing the perfection to unfold.

I think I finally figured out my love for the movie, *The Wizard of Oz*. It is not simply my favorite lines: After the Good Witch informs Dorothy that she can indeed return to Kansas, and Dorothy asks, *"Toto, too?"* and the witch brilliantly responds, *"Toto, too."*

It is more that in my highest and grandest vision of myself, I am a wizard. Here is that vision:

We're off to see the wizard, the wonderful wizard of God at Safe Haven Chiropractic. He talks like a blue streak in one moment (or for hours), the next minute he's not saying a word.

So much love flows from this wizard, your houseplants can benefit from being in his energy.

Be sure you want to heal, because healing begins immediately upon entering his presence, *thru* the magic of Love. He reduces subluxations when he enters the room or even when he thinks about you.

He has discovered his mission and he shares his talents openly and freely, and he serves without condition—you can feel that the moment he comes into your space. He is a wizard of attention, focusing so steadily and lovingly on the person he serves at that moment. An earthquake could swallow up all the land around him and he'd still be standing there hopping on

Work toward our highest visions, and all remember that when we do, we automatically help each other realize them.

one foot while giving you his all.

And boy can he give an adjustment! Can he find where it needs to be adjusted? Like nobody's business. Dr. Stew moves the bone, God does the healing — and he knows that. He is not the hero or savior. He doesn't attach to results, because he knows the results come only from above, down, inside out, and not from him. He allows results without knowing or caring exactly what they may be. He is a clean, hollow bone for God to work *thru*. And he'll love you *thru* heaven or hell, holding a vision of absolute and utter perfection for you, seeing you as pure Spirit and pure Love, for as long as you need to catch up. When you do you may not need him anymore and he's OK with that.

As a true teacher he's there as a guide, not with words of advice that do not apply to you, but with a loving touch, a hug, an agreement, a reminder. Whatever it takes. If you would enjoy being the person you were meant to become, go see this guy. He cares and loves enough to hold the space for your unfoldment and empowerment to happen without crowding in with his own intentions, his own expectations, his own agendas, his own ideas of what the truth is, or his own stuff. Work *thru* your own stuff in his presence and the process can occur with humor and lightness.

That is the vision I hold dearest for myself. I work toward it in every conscious moment. I project it in every conscious moment over the cosmic ATT system. My hope is that we all *work toward our highest visions, and all remember that when we do, we automatically help each other realize them.*

*We can move
onward and
look inward
and express
outward and
turn this whole
world upside
down.*

*Let's keep Him
around and
alive in our
hearts by tun-
ing ourselves in
to His channel.
A-Dios!*

Together we can watch our *Schmootz Brigades* sink into the quicksand of God. Together we can traverse the gulf of paradox and find our truths, and find ourselves in a paradise of connection and Spirit.

Will you join me? *We can move onward and look inward and express outward and turn this whole world upside down.* You'll look pretty funny doing a curtsy with your dress upside down, but think of the thrill for the rest of us! We'll walk around on our hands and play footsie with the world. Then we'll be in perfect position to give it a swift kick when it needs one. And it just might need one once in a while.

In the meantime, thanks for listening.

This book has been *brot* to you by God, and if you have made it this far, God is surely pleased—and probably a tad concerned about you. So He is certain to give you some special attention in the days and weeks to come. Try to enjoy that attention, because I hear God is thinking of directing His attention to another planet where people listen to Him. *Let's keep Him around and alive in our hearts by tuning ourselves in to His channel. A-Dios!*

♥   ♥   ♥

Don't take it personally. Live the impersonal life…flow and dance and gyrate in rhythm with all.

We really need to be with those who allow us to reach the highest highs, even if we also experience the lowest lows. Just another paradox.

P.S.

"Those are my principles.
If you don't like them
I have others."
Groucho Marx

The sun is shining, and my life is going thru the roof. There's no heat tape up there, so the ice dams are depending on Mother Nature to melt them—so is my heart. Thus begins the merry month of May, and some Beltane fires are definitely ignited in my loins—or at least in my shoulder chops, which are generally a little more expensive but well worth it. I can't tell you how pretty it is outside today. Even if you beg me.

I can't tell you anything, for that matter, which makes communication a pretty interesting thing. Interesting in its application as well as its theory. What is the theory? Well, e=mc2 is simpler. But don't take it personally. Live the impersonal life. That's a great idea for a book title, and undoubtedly that's why it's already been used. The impersonal life, the Innate life, begun at the dawning of time, manifested thru a circumscribed (even in Gentiles!) set of Twinkie atoms transformed to flourish, to serve, to give and to love. No attachments come with this email, and the anti-virus program needn't be installed, because in the impersonal life, we do not waste our time and energy with anti-anything. Everything is here and needs to be. We flow and dance and gyrate in rhythm with all. So it is in the month of May and always.

We watched *The Way We Were* yesterday, and the way we were yesterday has little to do with the way we are today.

But it did strike me that unrequited love is the saddest thing imaginable. *We really need to be with those who allow us to reach the highest highs, even if we also experience the lowest lows. Just another paradox*. The balance can be found.

Time and work and wisdom bring us ever closer.

In the meantime, people and relationships and love are indeed monumentally important, and require our greatest diligence, focus and energy. For therein lie the keys to the kingdom that teach us volumes about self and Self.

So I, peewee brain notwithstanding, or even notwithsitting, commit again and again to Love. I sit and breathe and whisper sweet nothings to myself, and somehow the raging seas of separation and carnal crapola are calmed. I feel the connection, feel the energy of love, and feel the feeling of feeling fine on Cloud Nine.

You can be what you want to be, all right, but you don't have to be a million miles from reality. That's where I find myself whenever I parade behind the *Schmootz Brigade* and end up playing a cello in a marching band or some equally unproductive activity. I'd much rather pray without ceasing, or play without ceasing, or even pay without ceasing, instead of paying the huger price of thinking without ceasing. I stop and notice the price; otherwise I just buy everything that comes along—and at retail no less, which is against my religion.

So where am I?

I feel ready. The voices of laziness, procrastination, smallness, judgment, poor discipline, and poor choices are gagging from lack of use. My brain continues to get quieter, *tho* somewhat cleverer in its approach, out of desperation.

Be desperate, oh great brain, your hold gets looser and looser around the throat of Innate, even if I have accepted the fact that you'll

*I guard
what goes out:
my thots,
my focus,
my actions,
my words.*

always be lurking around in the shadows, with occasional starring roles in my reality. But I've become diligent in guarding my treasure—my birthright of abundance, joy, unlimited creativity and possibilities, all that good stuff.

I no longer see the sense in guarding what I have in the material dimension, or in guarding what comes in (other than the right food, music, etc.) *I guard what goes out: my thots, my focus, my actions, my words.*

Only if I allow it can the petty thieves of doubt, attachment and ego-based desires chip away and ultimately block my good. *No mas!*

I am a child of God. I and the Father and the Mother are One. So are you.

And what I create *thru* my intentions is REAL in the spiritual dimension. My faith brings it back into my hands.

So I choose to guard what goes out and venture long and often into the spiritual dimension to meet my good and my God halfway.

MY DEAL WITH GOD

*I row
You steer.
I intend,
You manifest.
I stay out
of the way.
You create
my life in
a magnificent,
unique way.*

*Oh, sweet life.
I am a servant, a vessel
And my gifts are priceless,
Just as are yours.
I choose to remember.
I turn on the power.
I ignite the missionary flame
And hold it aloft
for the world to see,
To lambaste, to ridicule, to follow,
To love, to hate, to emulate,
Or to fear.
I am no longer afraid.
Mostly.
I peel layers of fear
And get closer to my Self.
I shed my skin,
Revealing the treasure within.
And I guard it well,
As a sacred trust.
My deal with God:
I row, You steer.
I intend, You manifest.
I stay out of the way.
You create my life
In a magnificent, unique way.*

Yes, folks, hold on tight to your dream, and guard it well.

LionHearted Order Form

Call 888-546-6478 or visit www.LionHearted.com

Title	ISBN	Price	Qty
Between Heaven and A Hard Place	1-57343-060-9	$19.99	_____

Shipping for Paperback books:

$2.50 per order, plus $1.00 per book   Shipping _____

Sub-Total _____

Sales Tax if purchased in Nevada   6.75% _____

Make check to "LionHearted" for $ _____

To pay by credit card (Visa, MC, AmExp, Discover):

Signature_____

Name (Print)_____

Card no._____ExpDt_____

Mail to: LionHearted Publishing, Inc.
         PO Box 618
         Zephyr Cove, NV 89448

Dr. Stew Bittman

An internationally acclaimed speaker and teacher, Dr. Stew Bittman has lived in Lake Tahoe for over 25 years. It is here that he has slowly recovered from his over-educated, uneventful mid-baby boom New York City upbringing and lives the life he always dreamed about. He has a deep love for the land, discovering God in the many flowering meadows and sun-kissed mountain lakes.

His reverence for Life extends to all humans on this planet, as well, and his mission is to empower one person at a time thru chiropractic. Dr. Stew has left no stone unturned on his own journey to facilitate each person's healing of themselves by rediscovering their own true nature and the doctor within.

Safe Haven Chiropractic is a healing center based on a donation-only system allowing all to achieve wellness. Stew has helped thousands of individuals and families to embrace their gifts, pursue their dreams and find the peace and wholeness (health) that already reside within. Additionally, he has traveled the world teaching the chiropractic principle, and has participated in six chiropractic missions to Central America, bringing that principle to life.

Stew's wife, Hillary, would like to add, "I think Stew would say that he is proud of what he's accomplished: a chiropractic practice that has literally changed the lives of thousands; a family that is very close and loving and that enjoys doing everything together; a balanced life which allows him to serve, to share his gifts and to live his dream. His mother-in-law thinks he is an angel. And, lest you think he sounds like a saint, I assure you that he is at least as full of schmootz as anybody else."

Dr. Stew can be reached for speaking engagements and seminars, for mentoring in practice and life skills, as well as for various audio and video products, at drstew@etahoe.com.